Diary of a Strike

SECOND EDITION

Bernard Karsh

UNIVERSITY OF ILLINOIS PRESS · URBANA · CHICAGO · LONDON

Illini Books edition, 1982

© 1958, 1982 by the Board of Trustees of the University of Illinois
Manufactured in the United States of America

Library of Congress Cataloging in Publication Data

Karsh, Bernard
  Diary of a strike.

  Bibliography: p.
  Includes index.
  1. Marinette Knitting Mills Strike, Marinette,
Wis., 1951.
HD5325.C62 1951.M37 1981   331.89′287700977534   81-10403
ISBN 0-252-00914-2   AACR2

Foreword

This is an unusual book, and still more unusual among works of nonfiction. Its subject matter — the daily events surrounding a strike of garment workers in Wisconsin — is the stuff of novels or motion pictures. Rarely is this story told by academics or journalists — and rarely so well as in this study. This work is not fiction, not propaganda, but reality: history as it actually was, and actually is.

Normally, when strikes are described, much is left out. Scholars most often take a perspective that is overly broad or coolly statistical. They lose the human drama, the sacrifice, the courage, the disappointment, the joys, even the humor. But who, after reading this book, will forget the moment when the company tried to have its winter heating coal sent through the mail?

Reporters for newspapers and television are better at relating the dramatic events of a strike, yet they too miss much of what a labor dispute is all about — the ebbs and flows, the subtle nuances of tactics, the improvisations, the countless decisions and countless details, the accumulation of small incidents that add up to a major confrontation. I think one has to live day by day with a strike to understand fully what is involved. Short of that, one can read Bernard Karsh's book.

Karsh has chosen his subject well. By focusing on a dispute in Marinette, Wisconsin, far from the nation's urban centers, he makes three-dimensional what would commonly be considered an "insignificant" event. Yet, as is so generously demonstrated here, the strike was not insignificant for the people involved. Far from it. For many of them, it would be among the most important occurrences in their lives — forcing them, in a way that few events can, to take full measure of themselves.

That Karsh is able to make real the human significance of a strike is a tribute to him as a scholar and a writer, and the people who will read his book — teachers, students, government officials, trade unionists, anyone who wants to know more about labor or the world as it exists today — owe him a great debt of gratitude.

Sol C. Chaikin
President, I.L.G.W.U.

Preface to the 1981 Edition

"Phil Draper," the union organizer, explained it this way:

We didn't want to call a strike — we played the string out. . . . we called in a conciliator, a federal conciliator. . . . We met all day Tuesday, we met Wednesday, and when we were all through hashing and rehashing everything, we were exactly at the same point where we started. . . . We were confronted suddenly, about 2:30 in the afternoon, with a situation where we were through. We were given a choice of accepting the Company's offer as it stood without any basic concessions which would permit us to live, or just fold up and forget about forming a union, or go on strike. There were no other alternatives. We didn't want to pull out. We wouldn't do a thing like that — having gone as far as we did and having the people depend on us to such an extent. We couldn't possibly accept the Company's terms because that would mean the same thing — it would mean no union in a very short order. . . . We had actual instructions from our Vice-President to accept any sort of a reasonable contract because it wasn't a good set-up for a strike. I was definitely uncertain as to the amount of people who would join us in a strike. I knew that a lot of people wanted a union, but I felt that they didn't want to fight for it. . . . We backed up so far that I don't know how I was able to sit up without falling over. We were willing to grasp at anything which would give us a reasonable opportunity to last for one year, hoping that within that one year we could consolidate our forces, we could build. . . . The absolute minimum was some form of union security and a wage increase. Then we called a recess and held a very hurried conference. The six on the committee and our lawyer and myself were agreed that the only thing to do was to call a strike. To do that meant calling a fast strike. Because if we didn't call it in a hurry, we would never be able to do it at all. . . . We were sure that the following day the Company would start working on the same people again . . . using all forms of intimidation or promises or both. It had to be done fast while it was real hot. . . .

This book is about that strike and the union-organizing campaign that preceded it. Almost four months were to go by before it ended with the negotiation of a first union contract. During its career, the strike had a momentous impact upon the participants and its effects spilled over into the whole community. The mayor said, "We never had a strike like that before in my memory and that goes back pretty far." A grocery store owner said that the strike almost tore the town apart. The local librarian felt that it was the worst thing that ever happened in Saylor. The employer was sure that "some of the things that were done during the strike were straight out of Russia. It was unbelievable." A clothing merchant stated that the strike had been a "terrible thing for the community."

The account which follows refers to the town as Saylor, in the upper Midwest. In accord with standard practice in social science research, many of the identifying names were changed. However, since the mid-1950s, when the original edition was published, the need to disguise informants has diminished. Actually, Saylor is Marinette, in the northeast corner of Wisconsin, directly across the river from Menominee, Michigan. The "Saylor Company" was the Marinette Knitting Mill and the union was the International Ladies Garment Workers Union, Local 480. The union organizer, "Phil Draper," was Harry Bovshow. During the later 40s and early 50s he was I.L.G.W.U. director for Wisconsin and manager of the Milwaukee Joint Board of the International Union. The manager of the Marinette Knitting Mill during the organizing efforts and the strike was J. S. Laureman, a nephew of the founder of the company and a member of the family which owned the mill and the very large department store that still dominates retail business in the town. He is called "Tom Miller" in the study. Walter Kohloff, called "Chuck" by his friends and referred to by that name in the story, was then a young organizer on Harry's Milwaukee staff.

It is not likely that many people outside of Marinette knew much about the events that tore at the fabric of the community. The small town in which the strike occurred is not very important except for those who live or trade there. The mill which was the immediate strike scene was not very important except to those who worked there or depended upon it for the general revenue it produced for the area. The whole situation probably had no perceptible effect outside of the immediate locality.

Then why write a book about the organization of a union directly involving about 200 workers in a small town far from the mainstream of American industry or unionism? Why be concerned with the events of a union-organizing campaign and a strike for a first contract in a situation which was really insignificant in the sweep of history? We were concerned with it because it involved human beings swept up in a conflict during which their lives and their livelihoods exploded about them. It provided a scarce opportunity to shed some light on the little-understood processes by which people argue and debate and sometimes fight to forge new social structures and new social institutions. We were concerned with it in an effort to understand how a union is formed at the shop level and the way the professional organizer goes about playing the key role. In short, the specific events in Marinette were not very important except to the people involved. But the knitting-mill strike was and is important because it tells us something about a class of events which has been repeated over and over again in our history. Workers have been organizing unions since before the American Revolution and something like what happened in Marinette has occurred time and time again and continues to occur. (For example, the recent Hollywood film *Norma Rae* depicts a union-organizing drive in a rural southern textile mill. Its similarities to the "Saylor" events are readily noted.) A close look at how the Marinette strike developed may be of some importance in understanding a little more about the complex world of trade unions, organizers, conflict and its resolution.

This study, then, is a report on the behavior of individuals in groups — what they believe, how they react, how they adjust to a conflict situation and its aftermath. Though the study design was based, in part, on a carefully thought-out statistical procedure, the results are not presented as measures of statistical similarities or differences or causal relationships quantitatively established. Rather, it is an attempt to describe types or patterns of experience in qualitative terms, in the same framework within which it all occurred. We wanted to know what happened to this small group of workers, living in a relatively isolated geographical area away from the broad currents of mass unionism in the large metropolitan regions. The quality and content of their lives in the mill was a major focus. We wanted to know how it happened that this group of workers, almost all women, came to reject an established way of factory life by joining a union and carrying on a bitter and violent struggle that lasted for many months and was felt for long years afterward.

Yet, though we were interested in the quality of those experiences and not particularly in the quantity, we did use a statistically valid sampling procedure and we did use measures of statistical relationships in analyzing our interview data. In addition to interviews with the workers, we talked to the employer, to the mayor, to leading businessmen in Marinette, to law-enforcement officials, cab drivers, grocery clerks, barbers, and all sorts of townspeople, both while the events were occurring and later on. And we examined in detail a file of more than 500 documents relating to the entire situation. And not least of all, we talked to the officials of the union who played the leading roles in the strike. It is primarily from the point of view of the union organizers and leaders that the details were gathered, since it was primarily the activities of organizers and leaders and the results of those activities with which we were concerned.

This study, then, represents the integration of various kinds of data secured in an effort to present collective bargaining and a strike as a process, from the inception of the union through its establishment as an integral part of the community. While the names of all persons and places were changed in the original edition, nothing else was altered. The events were true. The people are real.

The population of Marinette has declined somewhat, and a few new industries and firms have located there, but the town has changed very little since 1950, when the I.L.G.W.U. organizers first appeared. However, the principal actors have changed drastically. Certainly one of the most able union organizers and leaders in the greater Chicago–area labor movement, Harry Bovshow (Phil Draper), resigned from the I.L.G.W.U. to manage Gaylord Nelson's 1958 campaign for governor of Wisconsin. That, too, was a successful effort for Harry, as it also was for Governor and later Senator Nelson. In 1959 Harry was appointed to a senior post in the Chicago regional office of the Labor-Management Service Administration, U.S. Department of Labor. In 1975 he retired and emigrated to Israel, where he died in 1979. Former knitting-mill workers recall him with respect and admiration.

"Chuck" Kohloff retired from the union in 1979 after almost thirty years of service to the I.L.G.W.U. and now lives in Milwaukee. After the strike was settled, "Helen" continued her work with the Marinette local but on a much-reduced basis. Some years later she was assigned to another area of the International's activities and retired in the mid-1960s. Now in her eighty-fifth year, she lives in Michigan. Joe Laureman, the mill owner and manager called "Tom Miller" in the study, died very prematurely soon after the strike ended. The events surrounding his death are discussed in Chapter 9.

Only a few of the strikers are still in Marinette or in Menominee. Leona Bushek, Local 480's only recording secretary, was a member of the union's executive board until the end. In 1980 she was managing a small department store in Menominee and looking forward to retirement. Others in the local's leadership left the area after the mill closed, but a few active members are still employed in other firms and industries. Many have died; others still receive benefits from the International's retirement fund.

Until the mid-1950s the mill was the source of employment for as many as 200 workers. However, by 1957 or 1958 the press of competition from Korea, Hong Kong, Taiwan, and some European producers was already beginning to be substantially felt. Several of the mill's large chain-store buyers were not renewing contracts. Rather, increasingly, sweaters and other knitted items were coming from "offshore." Furthermore, the "high fashion" knitted dresses and other outer garments which had long been the principal Marinette mill products were no longer in style. By 1958, after the untimely death of the mill manager, his family appears to have lost interest in continuing efforts to keep the factory going. It had been closed for about a year when a New York–based firm leased the property and resumed production, this time with a line of much lower priced popular knitted garments, mostly sweaters, produced under a variety of labels for national chain distributors and retailers. The new operators also made some items as subcontractors for other knit-goods manufacturers. Employment was sporadic, with a reduced work force of fewer than 100. The new company continued to recognize the union and to operate under the terms of the extended old contract. This arrangement also failed within a year as orders continued to decline and production became sporadic.

After being closed again for many months, a syndicate of local investors headed by one of the mill's former supervisors leased the property from the original owners. This time a serious effort was made to reestablish the mill as a producer of very distinctive high-fashion women's apparel. A famous New York designer of topless swimsuits was retained to design a line of knitted beachwear, and a few of the old workers were recalled to make samples. Looking forward to renewed production and increased employment, officials of the Midwest regional I.L.G.W.U. office and Local 480 held several meetings with the owners to discuss union recognition and the future of their relationship. Very early it became clear that the new company would not agree to rehiring the union members in accordance with the seniority provisions of the old contract. Further, the new owners expressed a desire to be free of all union conditions for at least a year and also proposed that a new union-certification election be held then.

The I.L.G.W.U. leaders were in a dilemma. While willing to cooperate in any reasonable way to help the new firm get going and the local union membership to be reemployed there, they were decidedly averse to the company's proposals. The company seemed determined to operate without a union "until we get on our feet again." Union leaders talked about another strike but dismissed the idea as having little chance of success even if the company could get back into production.

The dilemma was resolved in late 1961 when the New York, Miami, Chicago, and Los Angeles showings of the new topless beachwear lines resulted in very few orders and the plans to again produce were shelved. The plant was closed and the new firm dissolved. In the mid-1970s it was again reopened by still another firm, this time to make upholstered furnishings for pleasure boats. A handful of the knitting-mill workers are now employed there and there is no union.

While it is possible that there were some at the time, fifteen years after the knitting mill was closed I was unable to find any former workers who associated their loss of work with the strike and the union. As before, some still said that the mill was closed because of mismanagement following Joe Laureman's death, that the Laureman family lost interest in keeping it open when no other family member assumed its leadership. Others pointed out that employment there, as is fairly common in the women's fashion industry generally, had always fluctuated with successes or failures of new styles, new designs, and new materials. The mill's principal product, knitted dresses and suits made of fine wool, had become less fashionable by the late 50s. Specialized machines at the mill were not adaptable to producing fashion items from the new synthetic fibers or switching to new fabrics altogether.

By the mid-1970s employment generally in this branch of the women's clothing industry had dropped to a small fraction of what it had been in earlier times. Only three knitting mills still operate in the Chicago and upper Midwest areas and none have union contracts. The I.L.G.W.U.'s largest knit-goods local, in New York, declined from more than 16,000 members in 1970 to fewer than 9,000 currently. American employers in knitting have found it almost impossible to compete with the imports from Asia as well as from Caribbean areas. One mill manager estimated that the wage level of American garment workers making knitted clothing would have had to be reduced to something like seventy cents an hour in 1975 in order for their wares to compete successfully with Hong Kong- or Haitian-produced sweaters. An industry characteristically composed of relatively under-capitalized firms using labor-intensive production methods found it nearly impossible to stay in business. I.L.G.W.U. leaders estimate that as many as 60,000 jobs in the knit-goods branch of the womens' apparel industry have been lost to offshore and overseas producers over the past two decades. One of the victims, in large part, was the Marinette Knitting Mill and the I.L.G.W.U. 480 members.

Not many of the former Local 480 members are still in the Marinette-Menominee area. Yet the knitting-mill strike remains a vivid memory for those still there, perhaps the most exciting event of their lives. More than half of the fulltime workers, including fence-sitters and scabs, retired with union pensions before everything stopped at the mill. Indeed, the oldest workers, who were at the same time the least enthusiastic about forming a union, became its most enthusiastic supporters and largest beneficiaries because of the negotiated retirement program. The local's files contain many notes and letters from retirees expressing deep gratitude to the union.

While nothing but memories is left of the I.L.G.W.U. local union in Marinette, the case remains instructive. The account of the organizing drive and the strike is still virtually unique in the literature of industrial relations. The intervening years have not contributed to our knowledge of such challenges. The activities of union organizers and the conduct of strikes remain largely unexplored. While there is a large literature on why workers join and form unions, I was unable to find a single account of how or why a local union, as a social institution, disappears.

Research is, in a sense, always a collaborative enterprise. Theories, ideas, and even methods are the products of the cumulative efforts of a good many persons, some of whom may even be anonymous to or forgotten by the researcher. This effort is no different. My debts to the people involved in the events reported here are very, very large. The study would have been impossible without the cooperation of the responsible union officials at both the national and local levels. The help I received from Harry, "Helen," Leona, and their co-workers was indispensable.

I am very grateful to Daisy Tagliacozzo, who interviewed many of the Marinette strikers and helped with the initial analysis of some of the raw data. My teachers, Herbert Blumer, Everett C. Hughes, and the late Joel Seidman, read the manuscript at various stages of development and contributed a host of valuable suggestions. I am particularly grateful to them for providing me with many of the insights I brought to the study and many of the implications I tried to draw from it. Phillips Garman, Milton Derber, Solomon Levine, Murray Edelman, and W. Ellison Chalmers, past and present co-workers at the Institute of Labor and Industrial Relations of the University of Illinois at Urbana-Champaign, and Jack Barbash, at the University of Wisconsin, all read the manuscript before it was initially published and in many ways helped to think through what I had written or proposed to rewrite. Barbara Dennis, then at the University of Illinois, spent more days than either she or I would like to recall carefully examining my use of words and expression of ideas. Her cheerful and patient editorial aid was invaluable.

My wife, Annette, was an indispensable companion through every step and every stage of this project. Her interest in it began when I exploited her as an interviewer. From that point on, her enthusiasm grew to nurture and, at many points, sustain my own.

I owe a particular debt to Harry Bovshow, the "Phil Draper" whose cooperation was always given with an open hand and, indeed, with enthusiasm. There could have been no study without his help. His death was a keen loss to all who knew him.

Some of the material included in this book first appeared in an article in *The American Journal of Sociology* and in *The Worker Views His Union,* a book published by the University of Chicago Press.

While I have put together many ideas not original with me and have solicited and accepted the cooperation and help of many persons, the final product is mine and I alone accept the responsibility for it.

Champaign, Illinois
March, 1981

Contents

Chapter 1	A Theoretical Perspective	1
Chapter 2	How It Began	16
Chapter 3	Why They Joined the Union	29
Chapter 4	Prelude to a Strike	46
Chapter 5	The Strike	68
Chapter 6	Tactics of Organizing	99
Chapter 7	Why They Strike — An Analysis of the Workers' Views	118
Chapter 8	New Relationships	135
Chapter 9	Four Years Later	154
Appendix	A Note on Method	161
Bibliography		169
Index		172

1

A Theoretical Perspective

Contrary to much general opinion, strikes are relatively infrequent occurrences in the United States. More than 95 per cent of the collective bargaining agreements in effect in 1955 were negotiated without resort to strike action.[1] Yet, the "general public" probably has a stereotype of a union as a strike-fomenting and strike-promoting institution. This is hardly surprising since strikes are certainly objects of much attention and are probably the most frequently and dramatically reported union activity. The far more routine negotiation which produces peaceful agreement is hardly as newsworthy as the group action, tactics and countertactics, and violence which often accompany strikes.

A strike may be defined as a situation in which a number of workers collectively withdraw their labor in order to secure some immediate advantage. It may take on a number of different tactical forms: a general strike, a sit-down strike, or a "quickie." The "slowdown," during which workers deliberately and in a concerted fashion decrease their work pace, is a tactical variation on the strike theme.

---

[1] More than 125,000 agreements were in effect in 1955. A total of 4,320 work stoppages of all categories occurred during the same year. See U. S. Bureau of Labor Statistics, *Monthly Labor Review*, LXXIX (July, 1956), 805, and U. S. Bureau of Labor Statistics, *Analysis of Work Stoppages,* 1955, Bulletin No. 1196 (Washington, 1956), p. 1.

An organized refusal to accept overtime work or an organized move to report for work at a prearranged late hour on a prearranged day or days may also be considered a "strike."

Reports and studies of strikes are profuse, but, with few exceptions, the treatment is either historical or statistical. Strike studies are generally concerned with historical events, programs and policies of leaders, frequencies of occurrence, and biographies. Social and social-psychological studies of strikes are few indeed.[2] Strike causes are most often found in the categories listed in charts or tables, with accompanying frequency distributions. Categories of causes list wages, hours, fringe benefits, union organization, or other working conditions.[3] Strike proneness by industries, strikes and the economic cycle, the strategy of "the general strike," the costs of strikes, duration of strikes, and similar treatments could fill a bibliography of perhaps a hundred entries.

Most of such studies seek to shed light upon the causes of strikes. Yet the causes, if there can be any fixed list of "causes," cannot be treated apart from the individuals and groups who do the striking. In a more profound and yet subtle way, explanations of strikes are not to be found alone in depersonalized charts, graphs, and tables. Nor are they to be found exclusively in the personalized biographies of the leaders of the labor movement. Since a strike is first and foremost a form of human behavior acted by individuals who are the immediate participants in groups, their causes are social as much as, if not more than, economic or historical. Persons caught in a strike situation carry burdens and play roles which no graphic presentation can adequately represent.

The ways in which men actually achieve concerted action, build up social organizations, and maintain morale in them constitute some of the most obscure and least understood problems in the whole field of

---

[2] W. Lloyd Warner and J. O. Low, *The Social System of the Modern Factory, The Strike: A Social Analysis* (New Haven, 1947), and Alvin W. Gouldner, *Wildcat Strike* (Yellow Springs, Ohio, 1954) represent the sum total of empirical strike studies as aspects of social behavior.

[3] For example, see U. S. Bureau of Labor Statistics, *Monthly Labor Review*, LXXVII (May, 1954).

human behavior.[4] In these terms, the strike offers a profound opportunity to the social scientist.

The best of all possible moments to achieve insight into the life of the human being is during a fundamental crisis when he is faced with grave decisions which can mean ruin and despair or success and happiness for him. In such crises men reveal what they are and often betray their innermost secrets in a way they never do and never can when life moves placidly and easily. If this is true for the study of men as individuals, it applies even more forcefully to the study of men in groups. It is when hell breaks loose and all men do their worst and best that the powerful forces which organize and control him and society are revealed. We learn, then, if ever, why groups of men must do the things they do and be the things they are. It is in these moments of crisis that the humdrum daily living of thousands of little men going to work with their lunch boxes and the prosaic existence of the big man in the top office reveal themselves as human dramas of the utmost significance; more importantly, behavior in such crises tells us the meanings and significance of human society.[5]

The essence of the strike lies in the behavior of human beings acting together; it involves groups and their relationships between and among each other; it requires planning and organization, the strategy and tactics of collective action; it involves the forging of new forms of social structure and sometimes the emergence of new social institutions.[6] It is not merely a cessation of work in pursuit of an economic goal; it represents an instance of social conflict in the form of a corporate refusal to participate in previously accepted social institutions. From its collective nature, the strike derives its power of coercion and the motives upon which it rests.

This study tries to capture for the reader some of the drama of the story. But for the study to be justified as a serious social science work, more is needed than the story. Facts do not speak for themselves; they

---

[4] Robert E. Park, *Society* (Glencoe, Ill., 1955), p. 31.

[5] Warner and Low, p. 1.

[6] Social scientists are apt to call anything socially established an "institution." I use the term here to apply to the established forms of procedure by which group activity is carried on. A social institution represents the formally established aspects of collective or group behavior. See Everett C. Hughes, "Institutions," *New Outlines of the Principles of Sociology,* ed. Alfred McClung Lee (New York, 1946), Part V.

have no intrinsic meaning or value. They take their meaning and their value from the way they are bound together with theory. That is, facts become meaningful as they are lifted from the level of the fortuitous and related to the more abstract. Facts, as empirically verifiable observations, are never gathered at random. They may be gathered in accordance with an unconscious preference, or they may be gathered in terms of some systematic scheme. For the scientist, facts are the meaningful products of efforts to relate them to a point of view. Science seeks to structure facts in some consistent fashion so that an orderly relationship is established between and among the facts. This logical structure or systematic scheme we call theory.

Since it is impossible for anyone to observe or cope with all there is to see in any situation, theory functions to narrow the range of observation and define the things which are relevant. It becomes a set of directions to the researcher, telling him what data he should be able to observe. It further tells him how to fit together the many items he observes so that he can hope to organize and systematize his empirical findings. And by no means of least importance, theory makes specific for the reader the color of the glasses through which the researcher was looking when he gathered his data.

The theoretical perspectives upon which this study was based are grounded in the contributions of a number of sociologists and the theories of collective behavior and social conflict developed by them.[7] The framework of this study can be summarized in the following propositions, each of which will be subsequently examined in detail and in the light of the story presented in the succeeding chapters.

1. Conflict is an indigenous component of the worker-employer (and especially the union-management) relationship. The strike is both an overt expression of the conflict and a method of expediential resolution leading to a new *modus vivendi* which permits both sides to exist in a relationship which is mutually dependent.

2. Successful union organization is dependent upon the existence of individual worker dissatisfaction and the transformation of individual unrest into collective or shared unrest. The strategy of the union organizer is designed to bring the workers together as a group to rec-

---

[7] The works of Blumer, Park, Cooley, Mead, Hoxie, and Simmel are the principal contributions developed in this study. I have drawn freely from their work in the areas of collective behavior and social conflict.

ognize the endemic conflict between their direct interests and those of their employer.

3. The behavior of an individual is largely influenced by what that individual assumes other members of his group expect of him. In other terms, it is the groups of which the individual is a member that yield the significant frame of reference for self-evaluation and thus, behavior.

4. If the members of a primary group[8] accept in a general way the values implied by the larger corporate body of which their group is a part, then the solidarity of the group functions to strengthen the motivation of the individual to follow the suggestions or commands of recognized leaders, both formal and informal, of the larger corporate body. The readiness of the primary group members to accept the generalized values of the larger body need not be strongly present in the consciousness of the individual, but some sense of generalized obligation and readiness to acknowledge the legitimacy of the demands of the generalized larger body must exist.[9]

5. Workers in the same objective situation will respond differently to the appeals of union organization and strike action. Some will join a union enthusiastically, others reluctantly or not at all. Similarly, some will strike without hesitation, others with considerable reservation, and still others not at all. The decision is largely influenced by the ex-

---

[8] "By primary group I mean those characterized by intimate face-to-face association and cooperation. . . . It is a 'we'; it involves the sort of sympathy and mutual identification of which 'we' is the natural expression. One lives in the feeling of the whole and finds the chief aims of his will in that feeling." Charles H. Cooley, *Social Organization* (Glencoe, Ill., 1956), p. 23. Modern social research has shown that the primary group is not merely the chief source of affection and accordingly the major factor in personality formation in infancy and childhood. The primary group continues to be the major source of social and psychological sustenance through adulthood. For an elaboration of this notion, see Edward A. Shils, "Primary Groups in the American Army," *Continuities in Social Research,* ed. Robert K. Merton and Paul E. Lazarsfeld (Glencoe, Ill., 1950), pp. 16-39; Edward A. Shils and Morris Janowitz, "Cohesion and Disintegration in the Wehrmacht in World War II," *Public Opinion Quarterly,* XII, No. 2 (1948), 280-315; Elton Mayo, *Human Problems of an Industrial Civilization* (New York, 1933); Elton Mayo and George F. Lombard, *Teamwork and Labor Turnover in the Aircraft Industry of Southern California* (Cambridge, 1944).

[9] This entire proposition is developed from a hypothesis advanced by Shils in Merton and Lazarsfeld, *op. cit.*

pected or imputed behavior of those whose opinions the individual considers to be most important to him. It is also influenced by such factors as degree of work dissatisfaction, economic dependence upon the job, and the tactics of the union organizer and the employer.

The organization of a union in a workplace represents the formation of a new social institution. But, "institutions do not spring full-formed from the head of Zeus. Before they are institutions they are institutions in process."[10] They represent individuals in social groups who have come to be at odds with their existing world, who have developed new or changed conceptions of themselves, their rights and dues, who have acquired new roles and new or changed values, and who strive to satisfy the conditions demanded by what they consider to be a new or altered situation.

The formation of a local union represents a degree of revolt and a new attack on collective problems. It stems from feelings of restlessness and discontent on the part of persons facing frustrating, undefined, or anxiety-producing circumstances in the factory. The disparity between the hopes and wishes of the individual and the realities of the work situation makes him susceptible of being organized for action along new lines. Situations of social unrest are crucibles in which new shared perspectives are forged out of old ones.[11] Old loyalties, allegiances, and identifications are at least partially dissolved. Though the major existing values may not be directly challenged, their efficacy comes under question and the practices which stem from them come under attack. Thus, the union, as a social institution, typically emerges from conditions such as these.

Often, however, the condition of social unrest does not exist among individuals in a given objective situation. Individual unrest, frustration, or discontent represents a fluid condition which has the potentialities for differing lines of action. Indeed, the unrest is not social until it is organized; expressions of individual dissatisfaction need to be crystallized, defined, and focused. Most of all they need to be communicated and thus shared. It is in these terms that leadership plays a crucial role.

---

[10] Hughes, p. 227.
[11] Herbert Blumer, "Collective Behavior," *New Outlines of the Principles of Sociology, op. cit.*

The general function of leadership is to coordinate and integrate group action. The leader defines the often highly ambiguous existing situation for his followers. He emphasizes certain aspects and ignores others; he asserts specific goals and deprecates others. He looks at the situation in an organized fashion and communicates his view to those he would lead. If his interpretation of the situation is sympathetically received by his would-be followers, a shared frame of reference or a common way of viewing the situation is developed and unified behavior is possible.

The union organizer is this kind of a leader. He seeks out situations in which workers have become disaffected from the conditions of their jobs or from the plant society. Once he finds such a situation, he designs his strategy to organize the feelings of the workers on behalf of the more or less powerful, and perhaps distant, union which he represents. He employs appropriate methods, techniques, strategy, and tactics to bind the workers together on the basis of their common membership in the union rather than on the basis of their work tasks, their employer, or other common interests. He seeks to engender a "we" consciousness among the workers which expresses their new status in the still abstract and generalized union. He knows that the union members are likely to follow his leadership if he is successful in winning their general acceptance of the relatively vague goals which he proclaims. He also knows that without the support of those workers whose opinions of him carry the most weight with their fellows, the workers are not likely to accept his suggestions for action or his definition of the situation. To paraphrase Mills, the union organizer is a manager of discontent, an agent in the institutional channeling of animosity.[12]

But what general explanation might there be for the dissatisfaction in the first place? From what does the unrest stem? What accounts for the discrepancy between the job aspirations of workers and satisfaction of those aspirations? In substance, why is the worker-employer and the union-management relationship basically antagonistic? A clue to these questions may be given when we examine the authority system the worker enters when he accepts employment.

Economists have long recognized the difficulty of measuring pre-

---

[12] C. Wright Mills, *The New Men of Power* (New York, 1948), p. 9.

cisely what it is that the worker sells to his employer. There appears to be general agreement, however, that when the worker enters the employee-employer relationship, he promises to sell his services. Commons has put it in these terms: "What [the worker] sells when he sells his labor is his willingness to use his faculties to a purpose that has been pointed out to him. He sells his promise to obey commands."[13]

But this raises a number of cogent questions: What commands has the worker promised to obey? In what specific way or ways must the obedience be carried out? At what point in the worker's performance of a command can it be said that the command has been fully executed? Who decides which commands dealing with what matters in the total employee-employer relationship the worker is compelled to obey? An implied promise to obey is not the same thing as a promise to deliver a given amount of work or a given number of units of output. It is a promise to sell to an employer the *ability* or *potential* for doing work. A conflict arises between the worker and his employer when the latter attempts to transform services into a specified amount of real output. No bargain or agreement had been previously reached or could have been reached concerning the actual amount of work to be done, the time it should legitimately take to do it, the way in which it is to be done, the conditions under which it is to be done, or the multitude of other unanticipated and unknown variables which arise from day to day or even moment to moment in a highly dynamic system.

The conflict is expressed in the different terms which are used to designate the wage which is given by the employer for obeying: the worker refers to his benefits as "income" while the employer refers to it as "costs." To the extent that one is maximized, the other is minimized, and as seen from the standpoint of the other, these values conflict. Precisely how much obedience the worker has promised to give in exchange for his "income" or precisely how much obedience the employer can legitimately demand in exchange for his "costs" is not explicitly stated. Nor can it be stated in such a way as to anticipate fully all of the ever-changing requirements of either the worker or the employer.

[13] John R. Commons, *The Legal Foundations of Capitalism* (New York, 1924), p. 284.

In a real sense, when the employer hires a worker he is buying "a pig in a poke." Gardner has put it in these terms:

Actually to the employer the labor he purchases is not a simple commodity such as a sheet of steel which he can buy according to certain specifications as to size, weight, strength, and chemical composition, all of which can be tested beforehand, and which can be expected to remain stable. . . . Labor . . . is the ability of a person to do work, and . . . this ability may vary from day to day and may be affected by all sorts of things.[14]

Similarly, when the worker sells his labor, he too is acting without the benefit of a set of clear understandings of what precisely will be expected of him. In the absence of any agreed-upon standard, the employer legitimately expects and indeed exercises his authority to demand that the employee fulfill his implied promise to obey.

In substance, then, the legitimate expectations of the parties concerning both work and obedience are unclear and vague and fail to provide a necessary condition of stability to the worker-management relationship.[15] Thus, workers and employers develop separate and conflicting notions about what constitutes a "fair day's work" and a "fair day's pay." A production quota that the worker might consider to be "fair" is viewed by management as "soldiering on the job" or "goldbricking." What the employer might consider to be a more "efficient" production method is viewed by the worker as a "speed up." What the employer might consider to be a "slowdown" is viewed by the worker as the absence of an adequate incentive system. What the worker might consider to be "pushing around" by a supervisor is viewed by management in terms of the requirement that employees follow instructions so that the company can "get out the work." And what the worker might conceive as a just grievance is viewed by management as a petty trifle or an irrational complaint. Further, what the employer might legitimately judge to be a proper order is viewed by the worker as "unreasonable" and caused by a supervisor "who has it in for me." The list is almost endless. Worker dissatisfaction typically stems from a situation which lacks a precise definition of what it is

---

[14] Burleigh Gardner, *Human Relations in Industry* (Chicago, 1947), p. 118.

[15] Gouldner has offered a similar formulation, among others, to explain the causes of a wildcat strike. See *Wildcat Strike,* pp. 162-65.

that he has promised to obey and thus of what is "right" and what is "due."

It is where such new or changed expectations of "rights" and "dues" remain as festering sources of discontent among individual workers that the union organizer finds his most fertile field. If he is successful in organizing the discontent, he stands a good chance of building a union.

Workers typically organize into unions so that they may seek to express a collective voice in the construction of a framework which will make explicit the unspecified and changing conditions under which they are willing to fulfill their promise to obey. Despite the unions' oft repeated assertion that the purpose of collective bargaining is to promote industrial peace, it is more fundamentally a step in the process of the control of conflict. Indeed, a significant aspect of unionism is the development of a process of control. Collective bargaining becomes the very method by which workers may achieve a measure of control and exercise it jointly with management.[16]

Whatever the immediate reasons workers may have for organizing unions, basic to them all is the objective of securing benefits and preserving existing benefits in an authority system which leaves unclear a definition of legitimate benefits and obligations. Or, having defined benefits and obligations and constructed a general framework which contains them (the contract), the authority system still leaves unclear the precise conditions under which the benefits are to be given or the precise conditions under which they might be demanded. The union, then, represents to the workers an organized vehicle through which they seek to limit the employer's legitimate expectation that the workers will fulfill their implied promise to obey.

Management seeks freedom to exercise its authority as it deems fit and freedom for business profit. It strives to maintain possession of authority to direct the business at its discretion. Organized workers

---

[16] Chamberlain lists a number of areas of union penetration of managerial control: finance; personnel hiring, allocation, size of force, layoffs, discipline, hours of work, promotions, safety, health, production in terms of the rates of operation and the setting of standards; distribution of the product; wages, job content. The process of collective bargaining is the method by which the union wrests from management its sole authority to determine these issues. See Neil Chamberlain, *The Union Challenge to Management Control* (New York, 1948).

seek an improved position to determine at their own discretion the terms on which they will accept continued employment. Organized worker penetration of the managerial function constitutes a threat to the logical goals of management and a direct challenge to its authority and discretion. To share the managerial function is to share and dilute this authority and discretion.[17]

But even more than this, unionized workers challenge the organizational framework and system of authority constructed by management in the running of an enterprise. The union challenges the accepted codes of efficiency developed by management and, if not the ethics of profit-making, at least management's system of profit distribution. It is not enough to say that unionization *results* in a shifting of authority within an existing system. A *sine qua non* of unionization is a modification of the system itself. Workers are organized for the implicit purpose of protecting and advancing their interests as workers. Implicit here is the notion that their interests as workers are different from the interests of their employer. Indeed, the test of legitimacy of a union is its independence and freedom from employer influence, domination, or control. I have yet to learn about a group of workers who organized themselves into something that they called a "trade union" where their conscious objective was to protect and advance the interests of their employer. To the extent that an organization of workers is independent of employer influence, it is best able to express the interests of its members.

None of this is to argue that the indigenous antagonism takes the form of a class struggle. Interest groups pervade all aspects of our society: political, religious, social, agricultural, business, and the rest of it. Modern American society can be viewed as an unending series of emergent and decaying interest groups which come naturally into conflict between and among each other.[18] The conflict with which we are concerned is between interest groups, not social classes.

The logic of the business enterprise is imposed by the ethics of the competitive system in which it operates. As our society is organized, the interests of organized workers who seek to protect and advance

---

[17] See Chamberlain, *op. cit.*
[18] Cf. Herbert Blumer, "Group Tension and Interest Organizations," in Industrial Relations Research Association, *Proceedings of the Second Annual Meeting* (Champaign, Ill., 1949), pp. 150-64.

what they consider to be their "rights" come into conflict with the interests of management to maximize its return on investment and conduct its affairs at its own discretion.[19] Yet both parties continue to be mutually dependent upon the continued existence of the enterprise and its solvency.

When management resists the efforts of workers to establish collective bargaining or to further their interests through collective bargaining, a strike, representing an overt eruption of indigenous conflict, may occur.[20]

The strike appears most obviously as a conflict manifestation. But its function is more than this. Within the framework of the American collective bargaining system it is a primary tool for resolving conflict.[21] At least three major implications are subsumed in this system. First, the conditions under which employees will sell their labor are determined by the group rather than the individual. Of course, it is true that individual leaders play important roles. But when speaking and acting in the collective bargaining process, the leaders function not as discrete individuals but as representatives of groups. Whatever authority or power they may have comes by virtue of having been endowed by the sanction of the group for whom they speak and act. Second, the system implies that the only way by which the terms of employment can be established is by *agreement*. Even where an agency of government enjoins a strike or a lockout or seizes a plant, the underlying dispute remains and is removed only when the parties themselves agree to remove it. Resolution may come in the form of agreement to submit the issues to a third party for adjudication. But nonetheless such a resolution still depends upon agreement to arbitrate. Third, the system implies that there is no universally accepted standard of fairness or equity regarding the demands or counterdemands of either party. A "fair day's pay for a fair day's work" is no guide for determining rates of output, standards of performance, extent of reward, or any other of the many issues which face union or employer represen-

---

[19] Cf. Peter F. Drucker, *The New Society* (New York, 1950), particularly Part III.

[20] Cf. Herbert Blumer, "Sociological Theory in Industrial Relations," *American Sociological Review*, XII (June, 1947), 271-78.

[21] George W. Taylor, "The Strike as a Socio-Economic Institution," in Industrial Relations Research Association, *Proceedings of the Third Annual Meeting* (Madison, Wis., 1950), p. 305.

tatives. In the absence of such standards, agreement is the sole criterion of fairness and equity.

It is within the framework of this system that the function of the strike takes its significance. In the event that voluntary discussion fails to produce agreement, either party may invoke a penalty in the form of loss of employment to workers through the lockout or loss of production to the employer through the strike. A strong motive power to negotiate agreement results from the threat of such loss. And in the case where a stoppage is undertaken, the strike again functions to bring about voluntary agreement, for only by agreement can the risks and costs of remaining unemployed and unproductive be ended.[22]

The strike, then, is the mechanism which produces that increment of pressure necessary to force agreement where the differences are persistent and do not yield to persuasion or argument around the bargaining table.

The alternative to such a system might result in the demise of the collective bargaining system as we know it; some form of coercion exercised by a supreme authority, whether it be a government board, an industrial relations court, compulsory arbitration, or some other of the many proposals which have been advanced from time to time, would supplant the voluntarism implicit in the American collective bargaining experience. Thus, the strike, or threat of strike, is the ultimate device whereby the competing interests of antagonistic parties are expediently resolved leading to a *modus operandi* which permits both sides to accommodate their differences and live with one another.[23]

---

[22] The World War II experience of the War Labor Board showed that without the right to strike as a motive power in agreement, unions and management, on the whole, found it more difficult, and in some cases impossible, to reconcile their differences. The 1945-46 strike wave which occurred after the dissolution of the WLB gives adequate testimony of this. See George W. Taylor, *Government Regulation of Industrial Relations* (New York, 1948).

[23] "The most effective prerequisite for preventing struggle, the exact knowledge of the comparative strength of the two parties, is very often attainable only by actually fighting out of the conflict," Georg Simmel, quoted in Lewis A. Coser, *The Functions of Social Conflict* (Glencoe, Ill., 1956), p. 133. Coser examines the implication of this formulation with respect to labor-management relations: "If the adversary's strength could be measured prior to engaging in conflict, antagonistic interests might be adjusted without such conflict; but where no means for prior measurement exists, only actual struggle may afford the exact knowledge of comparative strength. Since power can often be

These, then, are the major theoretical perspectives under which the study was made. The study of a single instance of a class of phenomenon does not permit the development of a general statement to cover all instances of that class. It would be a mistake for a union organizer who might read this case to try to emulate Phil's strategy or tactics. Similarly, it would be a mistake to conclude that Tom Miller's approach to his situation was right or wrong and that another employer in another situation should or should not follow Tom's example. Human experience and social situations are in a sense unique; they occur in a specific context and cannot be completely divorced from this context, cannot be separated from their past. Rather they relate to their totality, past and present. The events in Saylor are no exception, and it is not likely that they have occurred before or will be repeated in an identical context. Yet, the forces and processes involved in Saylor will be recognized as having been repeated, at least in part, over and over again in the development of the labor movement. There is no reason to assume that they will not play a similar role in the future.

Since the social scientist aims to study social reality, he goes to where that reality is found. He looks for instances of social experience which might make it possible for him to explain the general from the specific. His success depends upon many factors. Records are open to errors of perception, judgment, memory, and bias. There may be a special tendency to overemphasize the unusual. Subjective data do not readily lend themselves to quantitative check. Indeed, the representativeness of the specific instance studied may be challenged by other observers.

It would seem that the answers to these objections depend in some measure upon the researcher's choice of data, his ability as an observer and as a competent and accurate recorder. Perhaps most of all, his success depends upon his general knowledge of the subject area with which he is dealing and his ability to recognize representative instances of generic phenomenon. In all of these respects, the audience is at the mercy of the researcher. There is no final arbiter. The researcher's findings will stand or fall as they do or do not make sense,

---

appraised only in its actual exercise, accommodation may frequently be reached only after the contenders have measured their respective strength in conflict" (p. 135). Thus, conflict, rather than being disruptive, may be a means of balancing and therefore maintaining a society as a going concern.

as they are plausible to the audience for whom he is writing, and as they enable the members of that audience to glance behind the ordinary and accepted events of everyday living to achieve some new insight into the world under observation.

The strike of the Saylor workers presented a researcher with an opportunity to reach at least part way into the actual human experiences which constitute the live and actual social reality beneath the formal organization of social institutions. Further, it presented an opportunity to look behind the quantitatively treated data which, taken in themselves, are often not much more than symptoms of unknown causal processes. The usefulness of such a case study is enhanced when it is accurate and comprehensive, when it is directed toward facts relating to the whole process-of-becoming of the unit studied. It should seek to throw light on the processes, the causal factors, the rate and direction of change within typical social patterns. It is my judgment that the Saylor events do indeed provide opportunities to do this and it is for these reasons that it is presented.

2

How It Began

The strike took place in Saylor, a city on the Upper Great Lakes. Its citizens think of it as a "dead" town now, but during the late 1800's and early 1900's its port on the bay was one of the busiest in the country.

At that time it was a lumber town. Billions of board feet of timber from the virgin forests of two states came down the river to Saylor's twenty sawmills. In the timber drive of 1893 alone, almost four and a half million logs were cut into more than a half billion board feet of lumber. As many as twenty schooners could be seen at one time loading pine, balsa, spruce, and poplar from the docks which lined the harbor on both sides of the river mouth.

Men like Isaac Stephenson, Harrison Ludington, Jessie Spaulding, and Ely Wright came from the East (New England in particular) and became the great lumber barons. Then, soon after 1900, they left the cut-over land and the declining town to the former lumberjacks and the new merchant class — mostly people of French, German, or Scandinavian descent.

Much of the land settlement that followed the logging failed because the sandy soil and cut-over and burned-out land was not suitable for farming. Although reforestation was begun in the 1920's, the new young trees are not as yet producing high quality commercial timber. Only one small commercial sawmill remains in Saylor today.

The city, with a population of 14,000, is primarily a commercial trading center serving a population of almost 40,000 people. One newspaper, a single radio station, and very recently a television station service Saylor, and the town supports twenty-two churches and eight public schools.

Approximately 1,500 workers are employed in the city's many retail businesses. An almost equal number work in some thirty-five manufacturing establishments which range in size from very small handcraft shops employing as few as two to the large paper mill which employs as many as 600. An additional 750 workers are unemployed or underemployed and have been since the end of World War II, according to Chamber of Commerce statistics. Two hundred of the chronically unemployed are women. Wage levels in the city are about 20 per cent below the average for the state and probably close to 30 per cent below those of large urban areas in the same region.

Although there has always been some industry in Saylor, union members and officials regard it as a "poor labor town." Until World War II, unionism was confined to the crafts and trades organized by the carpenters, plumbers, painters, truck drivers, barbers, and electricians of the American Federation of Labor. The paper mills and a metalworking plant in a neighboring town were unionized during World War II. One chemical plant employing about 400 workers has dealt with an employees' association for more than a decade.

The Saylor Company, which produced an expensive line of soft goods, had been in operation for about 35 years and was the major stronghold of non-union enterprise in the town. Although the mill was organized as a corporation, all of the stock was held by members of one family whose business interests dated to the lumbering era. The Miller brothers, of Bohemian origin, opened a small retail store in Saylor around 1900 and operated as "pack merchants" for the lumberjacks in the backwoods country. By 1910 they had become general provisioners for the hundreds of lumber camps in the two-state area. One old-timer recalls that they "used to hit all the camps back in the woods and sell them supplies. Over the years they bought up a lot of real estate around here and made several fortunes."

Community spokesmen agreed that the Miller family represented the last of the local dynasties established when lumber was king. In addition to their retail merchandising business, they owned or controlled a number of other commercial interests, including the mill. At peak season the mill employed approximately 200 workers, all but fifteen of whom were women.

Leaders of the local trade union movement, the AFL Trades and Labor Council, considered the mill a difficult organizing target for at least two important reasons. First, the mill's work force consisted largely of married women whose commitment to the labor force was marginal, elderly women, and even some physically handicapped persons with few opportunities for alternative employment. In addition, the Millers enjoyed a favored position in the community. They were known for their works of charity, their generous donations to and support of the Catholic church, their influence in Saylor's political and economic life. The Millers "have always run this town," according to political leaders, business spokesmen, and union representatives. They go on to point out that although Saylor could be characterized as a low wage area, the wages paid by the Millers in their various enterprises were lower than prevailing levels in the community. The differential became particularly pronounced after the absentee-owned paper mills were unionized.

Officials of the Trades and Labor Council viewed these lower rates as a threat to union standards and tried to encourage organization among the mill workers. Although they found a few mill employees who were interested in forming a union, they did not know how to proceed. The local leaders were familiar with organization procedures in their own unions, but they were not even sure which international would have jurisdiction over the mill workers. Early in 1947 they turned to the AFL regional organizer who promised to contact the appropriate union officials in the area.

1947 — FAILURE

The AFL organizer relayed the information about the Saylor situation to Phil Draper, the union's director for the state, whose office was in a large metropolitan center almost 200 miles from Saylor. He assured Phil that officials of the Saylor Trades and Labor Council would lend whatever support they could to an organizing effort in the mill.

Phil came to Saylor in February to meet with the Trades and Labor Council officers and to gather additional information before he committed his union to an all-out organizing effort. He learned that if the workers lost their jobs for having joined the union or the owners decided to close the mill even temporarily as a tactic to combat unionization, most of the women workers would be unable to find other employment in the community. To protect the workers from possible recrimination or reprisals at the hands of a powerful and respected employer, Phil decided that any organizing campaign would have to be undertaken in secrecy. He was convinced that unionization of the Saylor mill would be difficult, but he decided to try it. He assigned Betty, a new organizer on his staff, to Saylor.

Betty arrived in Saylor on April 2. Four days later she reported to Phil that she was having trouble contacting the workers, even though one of the central labor body officials had provided her with the names of a few women who had expressed an interest in unionization. The mill was working on a two-shift basis and her contacts were on the second shift. She could not meet with them before working hours because of their family obligations, and evening meetings seemed to be out because the second shift worked until 10 P.M. and the city's bus service ceased at 10:30 P.M.

There isn't even one group that stops for a beer after work. Luncheons or Saturday meetings might eventually work out and meanwhile I'll start trying house calls. I've done most of my talking on buses so far — to the gals riding home from the mill. And since I made only one house call, I have only one signed card. . . . The bus driver is a good contact and he's got a couple of gals worked up whom I'll see next week. Other than the fact that the set-up men for the machines are making 70 bucks a week and as a result aren't much interested in a union, and the additional factor that the shop is about one-third on layoff, there doesn't seem to be much to add to the picture.

Phil answered that he was concerned about carrying on an organizing campaign with so many workers on layoff. He wanted to know if the layoffs were seasonal for the firm or the result of a general decline in business volume. "I would like to go slow," he wrote, "and not commit ourselves too deeply until we have a good line up of the situation there." In the meantime, Phil wrote to the State Department of

Taxation for a copy of the most recent tax returns for the Saylor Company to get some idea of the profit position of the company.

Betty shifted to house calls, but these too produced few results. Although she was making every effort to keep her work secret, she found that the mill workers were afraid that the company would learn of their union interests and that reprisals would result. She was unable to find any workers willing to take the leadership on behalf of the union inside the mill. Betty reported to Phil that "people want to wait, wait, wait, which I think is one of the major faults of a quiet campaign. They won't let me tell others about them wanting a union and so most of the people don't know a thing about it. They'd rather wait a few years until they consult their friends, husbands, brothers, cousins, and grandparents."

Betty concluded that many employees wanted a union but none was willing to identify himself openly with it. Sometimes she was told that others in the work force were interested in unionizing. But, she complained to Phil, the contacts would say, "Don't use my name, but I know that Susie or Mary or Jane is very much interested and go and see her." Because the campaign had to be a secret, she could not distribute leaflets at the mill gates or hold public meetings. After three weeks Betty reported that only nine of approximately 200 workers had signed union membership cards. Phil's initial reservations were confirmed.

We didn't want to put those people who had signed up in a position where the company would know of them, and we promised them that we wouldn't. So we couldn't use any of the open methods such as handbilling or meetings, and it had to be done on the "q.t."

Phil had hoped that a substantial proportion of the workers would join the union and that the campaign could be brought into the open. But such was not the case. Further, he expected that at least some workers would be willing to take active roles in the campaign and assume leadership inside the mill. Instead the entire burden fell upon Betty.

There was [Phil recalled] a great deal of sentiment for the union so that it would have been rather easy to organize the shop as I saw it — were it not for that terrific fear that made it impossible for us to come out in the open, and organizing behind closed doors can be a very difficult thing.

At this point, late June, 1947, the Taft-Hartley Act became law.
When the Taft-Hartley Act was passed and the people saw the blasts in the newspapers, a difficult organizing campaign became almost impossible. For about a year after the Act was passed I did no organizing at all. In Saylor the original fear of the employer plus Taft-Hartley made me — and I was the only one who made the decision — made it advisable to pull out before anyone was hurt, before it became public.

The decision was made. The campaign was called off.

1950 — THE PRELIMINARY SURVEY

Early in August, 1950, Phil heard from the Saylor Trades and Labor Council that a few of the mill workers were dissatisfied with mill conditions and wanted to unionize. But before he made another commitment on an organizing campaign, he wanted a survey of the local situation and a report on prospects for success there. He sent Helen Crowne, another of his staff members, to Saylor to investigate conditions in the mill and to sound out the workers. She also was to gather data on the mill itself — what products were being manufactured, how many workers were employed, what tasks they were performing and at what skill level, what wages they were receiving, and how they felt about the company, their fellow workers, and the idea of unionizing. As Helen put it:

If you send an organizer out and she comes back with the information that the people don't want a union, that their wage scale is good, that their treatment in the shop, their working conditions are good, and they don't want any part of a union, then the organizer doesn't stay there very long.

Through an official of the central labor body Helen arranged to meet with one of the mill workers whose husband was active in the central body. Helen not only wanted information about wages and working conditions but she also was looking for an employee who could take leadership for the union inside the mill. She wanted a natural leader of the work group — a person who was both courageous and calm and who was respected by supervisors as well as by fellow workers. She found such a person, another mill employee who dropped in while Helen was visiting at the home of her first contact. Helen reported:

I could tell by the conversation that Sue was very respected in the shop by the group; that when things went wrong she was not afraid to express her opinion and that different people in the shop came to her to tell her their troubles. I could see from what we talked about that management respected her opinion, too; when she complained enough, they would do the things she wanted.

The next evening Helen called on Sue to ask her if she would find out in a quiet manner what the workers thought of a union. She also asked if Sue would drive her around to the homes of other workers if a full-blown organizing campaign was undertaken. Sue had never heard of the union and wanted time to learn something about the organization. Two weeks later she wrote to Helen, telling her that she had discussed the matter with her husband, an active union member in one of the paper mills, and "he said that it was alright if you wanted me to drive you around to contact some of the girls. No one would know about it anyway."

By this time Phil and Helen had gathered enough information to have a fairly clear picture of the possibilities for organizing the mill. Many of the employees were dissatisfied with minimum guaranteed wage rates and low piece rates. Many felt that work was not equitably distributed by the supervisors and that some of the floor ladies divided the work so that a few favorites received materials easiest to work on and paying the highest rates. A few workers consistently earned more than others at the same level of skill. Most important, from the point of view of the organizers, was the fact that employees were found who were willing to aid actively in the campaign — an essential factor if the campaign was to be a success.

1950 ORGANIZING TACTICS

When Helen returned to Saylor several weeks later to begin the campaign, she tailored her organizing approach to the dissatisfactions of the prospective member and emphasized secrecy, personal contact, and the involvement of a number of workers inside the mill. Most of the early organizing work was concentrated in two long weekends. Helen described her method as follows:

Each of these members I contacted personally. Sue would park her car about a block away from the house and wait for me. We thought it would be best not to let anybody know who was taking me around. In advance Sue had told me all she knew about this person, what department she worked in, things about her personal life, if she was married and whether or not her husband was a union member and how many children she had, how much money she made and how long she worked in the shop, and in general what type of person she was and things like that. Each person had to be talked to differently. I would introduce myself and ask them to let me come in and talk to them for a few minutes about their work and a union. I would encourage them to do the talking and then through what they told me about themselves and their jobs, I had the answers for them. Having worked in a shop for fifteen years, I knew about what to look for.

A number of workers, fearful of layoff or other reprisals by the company, were willing to sign union cards only after Helen assured them that their names would be kept secret — a pledge that she scrupulously kept. One worker who had been employed in the mill for twenty-five years reported:

Helen came and talked to me. When I told her that I was making about 85 cents an hour, she pointed out that Tom [the employer] tried to keep wages down and how we would benefit from the union. I found out later that many had joined, but you'd never know it. You wouldn't know if your next door neighbor was in, it was so secret. I must say it was kept quiet. You'd ask someone if she belonged and you'd never get no satisfaction. They were scared of getting laid off. The Company had you scared.

Another woman who had been employed in the mill for eight years recounted how she had become angry when she found out that there was a move to organize a union and she had not been approached:

Helen had been going around for a couple of weeks and somebody in our department told me about it and I asked her for a union card right there and then and signed up. I never saw Helen till the first meeting was called about a month later. They were all very cautious in our department, and I was kind of angry that they left me out at first.

Another employee with eighteen years' experience in the mill recalled that Helen, when calling at her home, said that friends had sent her:

She never did tell me how she got my name. She asked me how much money I was making and when I told her she said that I wasn't getting enough for the work I was doing. I told her I didn't want my name used with anyone, and she said that she would keep everything quiet about people signed up. And that's the way it was kept — nothing was out in the open at that time.

Still another worker reported that she was hesitant about joining until Helen assured her that her name would be kept secret:

I never told nobody I joined — not until the whole thing was out in the open. It had to be kept secret because in this shop you just had to say "union" and you were fired. I'm sure a lot of the girls were scared to sign, but then Helen told me that about one hundred had signed already.

Early in her campaign Helen became aware of the importance of recruiting the male craftsmen to union membership. They were the most highly skilled workers and enjoyed much prestige in the mill. Several of the women whom Helen visited asked if the craftsmen had joined, and particularly if Bert had become a member. It became apparent to Helen that he was the key person in the craft section — the man to whom many others looked for guidance. But she was uncertain about what organizing approach to use with Bert since she realized that she knew nothing about the special skills of these craftsmen and the kind of work they did. When she visited him at his home, he reacted as she feared he would. He reported later: "I wanted to see a man. All she talked about was the women's work and didn't have any idea of what our work was." However, Bert told Helen that "if you have a 'good deal' to offer the boys, I'll promise 90 per cent of the craftsmen." Helen arranged with him to have the craft workers meet with Phil on the following Sunday. "When Phil came up here," Bert said, "that was better. He knew what he was talking about and knew our problems. We joined."

The physical separation of the craftsmen's workplace from other sections of the mill limited the contribution which these men could make to the organizing effort. However, their status as highly skilled workers lent much to the union's cause and made Helen's work easier since they, and particularly Bert, were willing to let her use their names in contacting other workers.

During her house calls, Helen found two women who had had prior union experience. Millie, the mother of five young children, had been a shop steward in a plant organized by the UAW-CIO in another city. She was familiar with the union movement in general and knew something about Helen's union in particular. Millie reported, "Helen came to my house and I told her that I knew that people couldn't be discharged for union activities. I knew we had laws against that."

Although the identity of most workers who had joined the union had to be guarded, some individuals were willing to work inside the shop on the necessary tasks of "feeling people out" and giving Helen names and addresses of those who responded sympathetically to the idea of organizing. Bert, for example, copied the names and addresses of all day-workers from the time-clock records. Another craftsman did the same for people on the night shift. Using a city directory and a telephone book, Helen made a file of all employees, arranged by the area of the city in which each lived. The file helped to systematize the work of visiting prospects with a minimum of lost time. The organizing drive began to pick up momentum. One of Helen's written reports to Phil during this period stated:

Yesterday afternoon from 5:30 to 11 P.M. I made house calls with Sue driving me around. That means 12 more cards for the whole day. This morning one of the girls dropped in at 8:30 and I invited her to breakfast. She told me that she had a contact in the shipping room and they are ready to organize. I called Bert right away, and he said that he would contact these boys today. I invited the girl who is driving me around and her husband and child to dinner with me so she can be free not to have to make the evening meal.

Thirty-two workers signed union cards as a result of house calls during the next four days. This brought the total to about fifty union members out of approximately 200 in the work force.

Phil was very much encouraged by the first two weeks of the organizing drive. He reported that

the first people that Helen contacted were not only ready to sign a card but a few of them, key people, were ready to make it known that they had signed a card and ready to help by going with Helen to other places or themselves taking the cards and getting their friends to sign. These were the overt bits of evidence that things had changed since 1947. . . . In those particular cases where the people said: "We'll sign cards but we don't want anyone to know" — that was done. In the cases where the people didn't ask that and wanted it to be known, we of course let it be known. It varied with individuals, . . . many were still afraid.

In addition to signing up members herself, Helen formed an "inside" organizing committee.

I got a couple of girls from each department and called them a committee. I tried to make them feel important — tried to make them feel that they were doing very important work and contributing a lot to build the union. They were responsible for getting names and contacting girls in their departments. I would call department meetings, and these girls would try to get everyone from their departments interested in coming to meet with me in my hotel room. . . . They would start by telling me all of their problems and discussing wages and conditions. I would let them talk, and I would act as if I couldn't believe that a company could let conditions like that exist. Most of the time they would be angry to think I couldn't believe them, and they would start explaining more thoroughly and bring in their pay envelopes, and that's what I wanted. In most cases before they left most of them would become stirred up and sign cards. And at the next meeting someone else would be curious and come to the meeting or tell the girls who were members that they would like to have me call on her. This worked beautifully — one group would boast, "All but two of my group are members" or "I have the most members in my department."

In this way a competition began among members of the "inside" committee to see who could recruit the largest number of persons.

Helen's tactics and personality impressed many employees and influenced their decisions to join the union. A machine operator recalled, "It was her efficiency — she knew what she was talking about, and she got results because she did it the right way." Another worker reported that Helen "was awfully nice — a sociable type of person. You felt free around her because she seemed like she was one of us. . . . She was just so friendly and she fit right in here."

As a result of Helen's tactics, news of union activity spread rapidly through the mill. By the end of the third week of active organizing, she had signed membership cards for eighty of the 200 workers. She reported to Phil that "the girls are beginning to forget their fear and are busy talking union all day. Since some 40 per cent of the mill employees were in the union, Phil decided that the time had come to bring the campaign into the open. As chief organizer in the area, he was responsible for choosing the right moment to formally notify the employer of the union's activity and to call the first general meeting of employees. He described the criteria on which he based his decision:

When we reached the stage where we had enough members, so that they were a large enough group where the company couldn't go ahead and fire one or two and stop the organizing drive, and also when they had gained strength and confidence from each other through knowing each other as union members, then we brought it out in the open.

At this point, Phil again secured a photostatic copy of the most recent income tax return for the Saylor Company.

Phil addressed a letter to Tom Miller, the plant manager, advising him that "a large percentage" of the mill workers had joined the union and informing him that he would like to "discuss arrangements to determine whether a majority of the workers want our Union as their bargaining agent." At the same time he arranged to have leaflets distributed at the plant gates, announcing the time and place of the first open meeting.

Up to this time the employer had given no indication to the union leaders or members that he was aware of what had been going on. However, the day after the employer received Phil's letter, one of the leaders of the "inside" committee reported to Helen that "the bosses have been holding meetings amongst themselves, and the department head in the inspection department has been telling the girls that the factory will close if the union comes in." In reporting this to Phil, Helen commented that she did not believe that such statements would hinder the union much, "as I have been telling the girls to expect this." Helen was correct in her assessment of the effect of employer statements. She and Phil were pleasantly surprised to find about 115 mill workers at the meeting held in the headquarters of the Saylor Trades and Labor Council.

Phil welcomed all those present — those who had signed union membership cards and those who had not. He began his talk by pointing out to the non-members in particular that nothing was going to occur at the meeting which the employer could not or should not hear. He described the structure of the union emphasizing its democratic character, and sketched the union's long struggle against oppressive substandard conditions, its present size of almost a half-million workers, and its continuing efforts to bring union conditions to unorganized workers.

He went on to say that a non-union shop was like a dictatorship where the employer had complete control over wages, hours, and working conditions, while a union shop was like a nation with laws and a constitution — the contract. He warned his audience, however, that he could not promise that the union was or would be perfect, "just as laws are not perfect," but he could promise that with organization would come a contract providing for job security, a grievance procedure, decent fringe benefits, wage increases, regular working hours, overtime pay, and the like. Through the union, he said, the workers would have a voice in determining their own working conditions and would be protected and supported by a very large and powerful international union.

He briefed the group on the organization procedure: As soon as the National Labor Relations Board held a union representation election, the local union would be formally organized, and stewards, officers, and a bargaining committee would be elected. There would be no initiation fee for those who joined before the election, and no dues would be collected until after a contract was signed. After that the local union membership would determine the amount of dues and would retain control over its own funds. It could, for example, set up a sickness-benefit program, as many union locals had done. He added that each member of the new local would be automatically entitled to receive a $500 death benefit from the international union.

Phil concluded with a warning — that the company probably would oppose the union and might even threaten to close the mill or move to another town. This, he said, was merely a usual tactic in an employer's anti-union campaign and the workers should disregard the threat. He encouraged the union members in the group to discuss the union with those who had not yet joined and promised that, whatever the obstacles and whatever the cost, as long as the workers wanted a union, it would be organized and it would win a contract.

3

Why They Joined the Union

Workers at the Saylor Company were not unlike others who have organized or joined unions over the years. Their complaints were widespread and, in most cases, very real — low wage rates, uncertain piecework prices, discrimination by supervisors, disorganized work assignments, and no seniority provisions for layoff, an important factor in a seasonal industry.

According to the workers themselves, the organizers had a fertile field in which to work. Helen and Phil did not have to generate grievances; instead they merely had to probe a bit for them during informal discussions. The organizers were quick to recognize valid complaints and lay the blame on the mill management.

An overwhelming majority of the workers were dissatisfied with their level of earnings. They felt that the guaranteed minimum wage of 75 cents per hour was too low and that the piecework system, which covered more than 80 per cent of all mill employees, provided no real opportunity to earn more than the guaranteed minimum. Although the guaranteed minimum had been increased from 45 to 75 cents over a period of four years, there had been no upward adjustment in piecework rates. The general effect was to dilute the incentive potential to the point where it had all but disappeared.

A worker, who subsequently became a leader in the union, commented:

The girls were discouraged about prices. The ones on piece rates had it the hardest. The rates were terrible, and they always had trouble and didn't make enough. I used to be a pieceworker, but I'm not anymore. I wouldn't ever do that again. No matter how hard you tried, you couldn't make out and you'd kill yourself trying.

Another worker complained about uncertain piecework prices:

I remember fighting about getting a price on a part. I make a sample and I always wanted the foreman to time me so that the foreman would have an idea of what price to put on the piece. I never knew how he arrived at his prices. Once I got a price on a part and I couldn't figure it out. I knew there was something wrong because I've worked on the same kind of part before and had a higher price. Once I would make one amount and another time another. When I'd squawk, sometimes he'd change it and sometimes he wouldn't. I'd never know what he was going to do.

A third worker described the effect of the increase in guaranteed minimum rates:

I felt the piece rates were not high enough. The fastest girls could make their time, but that was only a few. I tell you that when we were getting 45 cents an hour minimum, our piece rates were just the same as they are now. I don't think that was fair — do you? Look at the work you have to turn out for 90 cents. And when we couldn't make the bonus, we were bawled out each time.

Many of the workers became acutely aware of their relatively low earnings.

All of us have friends who are working in other factories around here, and my gosh, sometimes when we compared pay checks, we were almost ashamed to show ours.

A skilled maintenance mechanic learned that his wages compared unfavorably with those of friends working elsewhere at the same skill level.

I knew some of the fellows at the Trades and Labor Council, and I found out what rates were being paid around town and what rates were paid in other towns and what conditions in mills like ours were like in other towns.

Like in the industry generally, work in the mill was seasonal. Layoffs were the norm, and many workers felt insecure because the management had no systematic way for determining who should be laid off.

They just laid you off any way they pleased — just how they happened to like the people. Many of the workers joined the union because of the layoff procedure, especially those who had been there the longest. They figured they had a right to stay longest. I know I did.

Complaints involving the method of distributing work were common. Some workers felt that those who started work early in the morning got the "good work" — piecework which carried high prices. Others said it was the afternoon workers who were better able to "make out." For our purpose, it is unimportant whether the first or second shift workers had some advantage. However, it is important that the pieceworkers in general felt that work distribution methods were "unfair" and conditions were "bad."

A young operator, who had worked in the mill for six years, expressed a typical opinion on this issue:

You were pushed around a lot, and there was no system for doing things. People seemed always to be running around and nobody knew what they were doing. For example, one day before the union came in I got to work a few minutes late and found another girl on my job. I was sent to do her job. Well, this other girl didn't know the work I had been doing and she slowed up the whole line. They could just as easily have put me on my regular job when I did come in and not make all the other girls lose money because the other girl was slowing up the work.

A worker with fourteen years in the mill complained that she would "just get the junk and the old girls would get the good stuff" because the supervisor played favorites.

Another explained that often she was scheduled to report for work midway through the morning shift and continue on midway through the afternoon shift. Frequently she was ordered by her forelady to give up her machine to an afternoon worker and move to another machine vacated by a morning worker.

I used to get so darn mad at my boss when I had to give up my machine to the afternoon crew. I couldn't make anything with the other broken machine. They had double shifts sometimes and not enough machines, and it just got me mad when I had to give up my good machine. I always figured that I was there long enough before that other woman came and took over; I figured that I shouldn't have to give up that machine.

Just as often, workers charged that the trouble was due to discrimination by supervisors who administered the organization. They felt they were being "pushed around": "Unless you were an apple polisher, you always caught it when you stood up for your rights!" Some workers claimed that discrimination by the supervisors affected earnings: "She'd favor one girl in the department one day and the next day a different one. She could set how much money you made by giving you bad work or hard work." A shipping room packer said that his foreman, a relative of the plant manager, took advantage of the workers:

He swore and cursed and called me a damn Polack. I guess he just doesn't know any better — he's just ignorant. He's Tom Miller's cousin and so he thinks he can get away with anything. When he knows you're dependent on your wages, he thinks he can push you around because you can't quit so easy as some of these married women who don't need the money so much.

A highly skilled worker who later became a leader of the new local complained that her forelady tried to interfere with her home life:

I used to ride to work with my husband at 7 A.M., and she told me one day that my husband should get a ride with another girl so I could take the car and bring some girls in with me. She was mad because I wouldn't do it. Not only that, but when I would bring some work up to her that she had given me and show her a bad spot in the material, she'd ignore it or tell me it was okay. And then I'd finish the work and she'd say it was no good. She used to treat everybody that way.

Some complained that their foreladies were "mean and crabby" or that the foremen were "nasty" or "high-strung." Others complained that their supervisors either ignored them or spoke to them in a gruff manner.

She just passes me by and once in a while she would get cross. She could have been more pleasant and it wouldn't hurt her. She doesn't have many friendly words like a boss should have. But I'm not the only one she treats that way so I don't feel too bad. If she don't like me, I don't like her either.

A worker volunteered the opinion that the 1947 organizing drive had failed "because the bosses pampered some of the workers so they wouldn't want a union."

Many workers were convinced that there was nothing they could do about their work problems because the supervisors paid no attention to their complaints. "They wouldn't listen to you. They'd say like they said so many times — 'If you don't like it, you know what you can do. There's the door.' "

A machine operator felt that her seven years in the mill entitled her to an opportunity to get work which paid higher earnings.

I was working on one line at one time and not making enough. I wanted to get switched to another line where you made more. I went up to the boss and asked for the transfer. She said that some good operators had to stay on where they were and I didn't get anywhere.

Another worker operated a large steaming machine in the pressing room.

I've had trouble with piece rates and hourly rates, and I never got anything done. I asked the assistant superintendent to try to get me a raise on different parts that were coming through that were harder to work on, and he'd say that he couldn't do anything and that he had to talk to the superintendent and that's the last I'd ever hear about it. They'd always come back with "This job is set up for a woman." He meant that I ought to be satisfied with whatever I made because they were doing me a favor by letting me have the job. The truth is that I turn out much more work than any woman who was ever on the job before I got it, and they knew it.

A skilled worker related that he became convinced that a union was necessary as the result of an experience he had with the mill superintendent:

Most of the fellows were having trouble with one thing or another for a couple of months. Those of us in our department are young fellows who were out for the money and could work hard and fast for it, and we were doing most of the griping. One day we were asked to work on Labor Day at straight time earnings, no overtime, and we had a bad day. It seemed like things went wrong all day, and we didn't even make our guarantee of a buck-twenty. I made a dollar-fourteen an hour that day. We were mad that the company wouldn't pay us for the holiday, and now with things just seeming to go wrong all the time or the machine needing too many setups, this just added to it. So the six of us went to see the superintendent. We went in together. We knew that once before a group of girls in another department had had a gripe and went to the boss in a group and they were all canned for it. But we went anyway. He didn't do anything for us for the Labor

Day pay. I was doing most of the talking, and he said he wouldn't pay us our minimum because he said we weren't working hard enough. I told him that his desk was only a few feet from my machine, and he was there all the time watching how hard I was working and he knew that such a statement was a lie. He burned me up with that stuff. Then he said to me, "John, if you don't like it, there's the door." In my mind, that's where the union started for me.

A skilled worker with fifteen years' experience in the mill had had many problems over the years but had learned, she said, that it was fruitless to talk to her immediate supervisors. She had come to feel that going over their heads to the employer would have meant loss of her job "within a week's time." A machine operator with ten years in the mill complained to her forelady that her earnings were low because she was not being given enough work to do. The forelady replied, "Well, if you don't like it, you know what you can do." The worker commented, "I never complained again."

Unionism in Saylor's other large establishments was an important factor in the mill situation. Though very few mill workers had had any prior direct experience with unionism, most of them were familiar with the idea in a very general way, for most of the women workers had husbands, brothers, or fathers who were union members elsewhere.

One worker, for example, who became a member of the "inside" organizing committee, reported that the union was the first with which she had had any direct experience. Her husband convinced her that she should join and help with the organizing.

My husband is a union member — has been for years. He's 100 per cent for union and always was, and he encouraged me. He told me to go out and work with the organizers because the union was trying to do the right thing.

The husband of a shipping room packer also encouraged his wife.

He wanted me to be in the union. He could see what the union had done at his place. They had nothing down there before the union came in and he knew that our conditions were bad.

Others made similar comments:

My husband has been vice president of the union in his paper mill. He said you get protection and the union has good leaders and it's a good union. He said it all depends on the union and the leaders you get and that I couldn't go wrong.

I never knew much about unions from my own experience, but I always believed in unions and I wanted to get one in the mill for a long time. I come from a laboring family. There's more dignity in a union; it makes you feel that you can stand on your own feet. My father is a union member from way back. My brother once tried to organize a union at the Millers' store and lost his job for it.

I've always been for unions. My husband is a union man. He drives a truck for the city. When he first got a union in his work — when they were first organizing the truck drivers — I lived union for a time. He's all wrapped up in it. He reads all the union papers that come to the house all the time. He has a brother who worked for the railroads, and he remembers when it was a crime to join a union. My brother-in-law talks about those things when he comes over.

Some of the in-plant leaders had been members of unions in other places of employment. A few had been officers or members of committees. Millie had been active in organizing a union in another plant in the community.

I was on the organizing campaign at a furniture factory. That was a plant like ours before the union came in. The working conditions were sloppy and we got many improvements — better wages, working hours were better, and paid holidays.

She was one of the first volunteers on Helen's "inside" committee and later became a top officer of the local.

Although the majority of workers said they joined the union because of dissatisfaction with wages and working conditions, fortified by encouragement from union-member relatives or close associates, a substantial minority related that they joined because others were joining. The social pressure of the informal group was the conscious deciding factor for about a quarter of the union members. Conformity became the central motivation.

Elaine had been employed in the mill for twenty-seven years. She knew nothing about the budding union until the first open meeting was held, almost two months after Phil and Helen began the campaign. "I went to the meeting because some of the other girls were going. When I got there, somebody gave me a card and I signed it. I just wanted to be with the girls. That's why I joined." A woman with fifteen years in the mill explained, "I figured that if everybody wanted to go into it, I'd go along with them."

A comment by one of the oldest mill employees illustrates some of the doubts and fears faced by the older employees.

After the union was started, Millie and Sue came to see me and promised me the world with a fence around it — good money, eight-hours-a-day work, new girls wouldn't be kept while I was laid off. It was tempting. The company thought I didn't sign up until after the strike, but I signed almost nine months before. I was scared, but my family talked to me. My brother worked at the glove factory, and he discussed the union with me. That made me feel better when I was worried that the boss would find out. When Helen came to see me, I was still afraid. I'm over sixty and I've been there almost forty years, and where could I get a job in this town if I lost this one. But I told Helen that if all the rest sign up, then I will too. And when I found out after the first big meeting that most of them were members, I joined.

In most cases, it was not one reason alone which convinced a mill worker to respond sympathetically to the organizers' appeals. Most often it was a combination of reasons: dissatisfaction with rates of pay or organization of the work, inability to satisfy complaints, complaints against supervision, and the insecurity of job tenure in an industry characterized by seasonal employment. Some workers were encouraged by relatives and others by friends. They came to believe that the union would eliminate the causes for their unhappiness in the mill.

"FENCE-SITTERS"

Thirty-two of the Saylor Company employees were labeled "fence-sitters" by the union members. They were the ones who were most indecisive about joining the union. Some joined during the first weeks of the organizing campaign, withdrew, and finally voluntarily rejoined at a later date. Others waited to join until the final stages of the campaign.

The fence-sitters had a number of characteristics quite different from the other union members. Very few had husbands, brothers, or other family members who were union members. The percentage of primary wage-earners among them was four times as high as for the new unionists. On the average they were almost seven years older and had been working in the mill almost twice as long. In sharp contrast to the other group, more than three-quarters of the fence-sitters explained that they joined the union (or withdrew membership and rejoined) because they "wanted to be with the girls." The pressure of the informal work group was the conscious decisive factor among only about a quarter of the others.

Several of the fence-sitters were caught up in a web of individual conflicts which were very difficult for them to solve. An interview with one such worker illustrates the confusion resulting from loyalties to her co-workers in conflict with loyalty to and fear of her employer. At first she decided to remain neutral in the growing dispute. When it appeared that the union would emerge as a going concern, she joined.

The interview took place in the living room of her home. It was early evening and the room was quite dark except for a single small lamp on a corner table. The furniture was old and threadbare, but, like the rest of the room, spotlessly clean. The worker was sixty-five years old. She related her experience in a soft voice, at times almost inaudible, and she often would sigh as tears came to her eyes. During the three and one-half hour interview, she told of the unhappiness in her life. Her husband had been ill for many years before his death, and during this time she was the sole support of her family. She had had several major illnesses and at times her family was almost destitute. Since it had been necessary for her to work most of the time, her parents had cared for her children, and she had hardly gotten to know them. She was a native of Saylor and had known and respected the Miller family all her life.

My sister had been working at the Millers' store for fifty-seven years. I can say this much about the Millers — you can't find better people anywhere in the world in time of need. When my husband died, the undertaker told us the bill was all paid for. We found out after that the Millers had paid for it. They gave me the living room set that you are sitting on when I got married. My folks knew the family many years ago, and I had always heard nice things about them. I worked at the five and ten cents store in town for twenty-five years, and about ten years ago when I was fifty-five, I fell down in the store and hurt my arm. Then they fired me. That's when Tom Miller gave me a job in the mill. I don't know what I would have done if he hadn't hired me — there's no place else around here that will hire a fifty-five-year-old woman. When the organizers came to see me to join, I was in between two fires and didn't know what to do. I told them that I couldn't do it until I was sure that I wouldn't lose my job — until the union had a contract. But I would have liked to join because so many of the other girls did. One of my nephews is Tom Miller's close friend, and my sister had been working in the store for so many years and I was afraid that they would make it bad for her. She called me several times and begged me not to join. My son and son-in-law are in unions and are all for it. My son is a truck driver. I joined just before the strike was settled because by that time just about everybody else was a member.

Other fence-sitter cases were less dramatic but contained similar factors. A fifty-five-year-old woman who supported her disabled husband was reluctant to join when Helen approached her.

I didn't think it would work out because the Millers were so much against the union. I didn't know much about unions at all before it all started here, and I joined three weeks after the strike began. I didn't join right away because I thought the Millers wouldn't like it and maybe the union would lose and then where would I be. But after I found out that all the other girls in my department were joining, I did too.

The claims made by the organizers and the counterclaims advanced by the company created conflicts for some workers. Following the leadership of others brought some relief.

There was an awful lot of confusion. You don't know what to say or think. First you hear the union, and then Mr. Miller would come and tell you something else. You really don't know what to do. I wanted to do what the rest of the girls did — that's why I waited.

A cutter hesitated when asked to join because her father did business with the Miller family.

To my father the Millers have always been very good, and Tom Miller had never done anything to me. My mother didn't want to hurt my dad's business, so I joined only when the strike was almost over. I joined mostly because all of my friends and my aunts joined.

A middle-aged worker, whose husband had a small woodworking business in Saylor, was reluctant to join because, like so many other fence-sitters, her family was dependent upon her earnings to supplement the family income and she feared employer reprisal. She became a member after she had been temporarily laid off and the union had succeeded in helping her return to work.

There was so much talk going on in the plant that I just couldn't make up my mind. That's why I stayed neutral. I wasn't going to hurt either side. Then I was laid off and the union took my case and went to Miller and told him about my seniority rights. They told him he had to get me back to work. I thought that if they bother about somebody who isn't even a member of their union, they must be all right. I joined right then and was sorry that I didn't join sooner.

Some twenty-five of the fence-sitters joined the union twice — once early in the organizing campaign and again much later. In the interval they had participated in a withdrawal movement suggested by the employer and organized by members of his supervisory staff.

A worker who subsequently became a leader of the local was one of these. She was a divorcee and the sole support of her three young children. She had never before had any experience with unions. It was the fear of losing her job that influenced her to withdraw from membership.

Miller said he would give us a steady job and that we would not lose our jobs if we leave the union now. He would always give speeches every other day. He promised us steady work and steady jobs — that's all. And then he gave us fifteen cents an hour extra while the union was organizing. I guess it was kind of a bribe. Then he had one of the people in the department circulate a petition, and two of them came to my home to talk to me. I signed the petition. I was afraid that I would lose my job. . . . Many others signed the petition too — for the same reason. We were scared to lose our jobs. We were just scared stiff.

She later rejoined when her co-workers did.

Another worker, when asked why she withdrew, replied:

Because everybody else dropped out. . . . It was just that most of the girls dropped out; we had no particular reason. When they preached us that we don't need a union and that we will get all these things without it — well, we just dropped out. When they went on strike later, we signed up again because all the others signed up too. But I guess I was influenced by what Mr. Miller said. I thought we can trust him; he's an honest man, and it was just that a lot of bad things that went on in the mill he didn't know about. If you have never belonged to a union, you don't know its true meaning and its true value — you just don't know what to do. I didn't dislike the people from the union, but I can imagine that it's pretty hard for Mr. Miller. If you run a concern, you don't like outsiders to run your business for you. I could sympathize with him. We just dropped out all about the same time when we heard that Mr. Miller was not for the union and that he thought it wasn't necessary.

A middle-aged hand worker, who had been employed by the company since 1926, also joined early in the campaign and later withdrew.

When it started out, I was in favor of it, but my department couldn't make up their mind and we decided to stick together. We signed up, but then the whole bunch in my department withdrew and so did I. I guess they just thought the union would not get in. Some were in favor of it and some were not. But we all withdrew and I withdrew because all the others did. It's silly to even say it, but if you work with a bunch, you like to stick together. When the petition went around, I just signed because all the others had signed before me. . . . I joined again during the strike; most of my girls did the same thing. . . . You never know quite what's right and what's wrong, and if you got a bunch together, you just like to do what they are doing.

A statement that was heard frequently among the fence-sitters — "Everybody else in my group was doing it and you had to be with the majority" — emphasizes the compelling factor which led them to join the union.

NON-JOINERS

Twenty-nine employees out of the total work force of approximately 200 were not union members when the strike ended. They had resisted all efforts of the professional organizers and their co-workers to induce them to join. More than half of them worked in two departments of the mill. Whereas all of the other departments were represented either in the union leadership group or in the larger "inside" organizing committee, Helen and Phil had never been able to find anyone in either of these departments who was willing to assume a leadership role in the organizing effort.

It was not easy to interview the non-joiners. They had developed a very tightly knit group during the strike, and their leaders resented the efforts of an "outsider" to probe for the reasons for their behavior. Although efforts to get cooperation from their leaders failed, some contacts were established with individual members. Only five non-joiners agreed to be interviewed.

Some data were secured for the group as a whole. The non-joiners were, on the average, almost ten years older than either the fence-sitters or the rank-and-file members and, as a group, had the longest tenure in the mill. Further, almost 90 per cent of them had no other means of support, as compared with 73 per cent of the fence-sitters and 45 per cent of the rank-and-file union members.

Pete, for example, was one of the skilled craftsmen who were among the first to join the union, but he withdrew a few weeks later and stayed out. He had worked in the mill since 1912 and had a pronounced physical handicap.

I went down to the first meeting they held with all the skilled tradesmen. We all went down to the union hall. That Draper spoke and that's what started me off. He didn't care about us or the Millers. Because if he did, he wouldn't have told us what the union was asking for like he did because he knew as well as I did that Tom Miller couldn't meet those demands. He talked like a Communist right from Russia. But I signed a membership card because all the rest of the skilled men did too.

His initial reservation about the union was intensified as the organizing campaign gathered momentum. Unlike the skilled men who remained loyal to the union, Pete perceived the situation in terms of his handicap. When he learned that his employer opposed the union, he felt he could not afford to risk loss of his job: "Where could I ever get another job around here if I lost my job at the mill? Who would ever hire a cripple like me? I'm going to be sixty-five years old." In this light, his appraisal of Helen and Phil continued to be negative. The success of the organizing drive, he said, was due entirely to

the outside agitators who came in here to stir up trouble. Most of the women who joined had husbands who were union members or were women who didn't have to work for a living, and the agitators stirred them up — got them all riled up. Those organizers were Communist Bolsheviks and that's their job. Every union member they get signed up means more money in their pockets. They're professional pickets. They were paid to come in here from the outside and do what they did. They don't care about the workers in the shop or about Miller.

Pete related that Mr. Miller had addressed several meetings of the entire work force and had claimed that the organizers were outsiders whose objective was to get dues from those whom they were able to induce to join the union. Further, he reported that Mr. Miller told the employees that "there was nothing the union could get for them that he wouldn't give us without a union — that the union couldn't do us any good because he would take care of us." Pete said that he believed his employer "because he's a good Christian and always treated me fine."

Joe was another worker who remained out of the union. He had been employed as a mechanic in the mill for almost forty years. He was responsible for the mechanical maintenance of the machinery and worked in semi-isolation from the other employees. Like Pete, he very much admired the Miller family and Tom Miller in particular.

Tom is the nicest boss I could imagine. He always treated me fine, and I never had no cause to complain. I always made good money. Tom is a graduate of Notre Dame, but he never put on any airs and is just as common as you or me and acts as if he never had no more education than you or me. He always tried to give the people their work. He'd keep them on in slack times just to see that they made some money.

Joe felt that unions, in general, were useful organizations. However, he could see no justification for a union in the mill because of the seasonal aspects of the industry.

Unions are wonderful things. They do a lot of good for people. It's not exactly like a church, but it makes people feel that they are together. A smart union leader with a good personality could get a lot more for a worker than he could get for himself. But it all depends on what factory you're talking about. A union is no good in the mill because the work is seasonal. Maybe you work for six months of the year and then you're laid off for six months unless you're lucky like me. I've been working steady all year around for many years now. The company loses money for six months of the year, and they try to make it up the other six months. That's the way this business is run and a union can't help that. A union is a good thing like in the paper mills where the men work eight hours a day, seven days a week, and fifty-two weeks a year. I'm all for it in a place like that.

He felt that the grievances of the women workers were unjustified.

They were getting 75 cents an hour whether they worked for it or not. I know a lot of them said that they couldn't make more money than that. But they could have made a lot more if they wanted to work. But any time you'd look over on their side, they'd be standing around doing nothing or be down in the can talking. Nobody could make money if they didn't work for it. They just wanted something for nothing — especially the young ones. They think the world owes them something that they don't have to work for. If they were dissatisfied, they should have quit and gone somewhere else.

Joe found it difficult to understand how the organizers had turned the women's grievances to their own advantage.

That Phil Draper cast a spell over them. He's one of the slickest men I ever saw. He had them women going so that they would do anything he'd say — anything! He told them all kinds of stories and lies and they believed them all. They brought in a second woman organizer during the strike, and she had the foulest mouth I ever heard on a woman. She talked as if she had her mouth full of —— all the time. She acted just like a —— Communist.

Reactions of other non-joiners were similar, although the bitterness toward the organizers was not so pronounced in all cases. A sixty-one-year-old divorcee stayed out of the union because of her dependence upon her employer. "I needed the money to pay taxes and the upkeep on this house. Also I was making payments on a new refrigerator and TV set and needed the money. That's the way it was with almost all of us — we all needed the money." She joined the union immediately after the strike settlement but before the negotiated union shop agreement became effective. "I felt the union was here to stay and I might as well get in with them."

Ruth was sixty-eight years old. The other six workers in her department were all over sixty-five years old, and none of them joined the union. Ruth had been widowed twenty years before and supported herself. She felt that she could not afford to risk loss of her job by joining the union since she was trying to build up maximum social security credits toward retirement. "I was afraid that if I joined and got fired, there would be no way for me to live. I would have to go to an old people's home."

The interviewer found only one worker whose negative reaction to the appeals of the organizers stemmed from experience with other unions. He drove the mill's delivery truck and worked in isolation from other employees. The union's cause was justified, he said, for those who did join. "Nobody could have gotten them into that union unless they were dissatisfied." He had heard on several occasions that the large majority of women workers were unhappy with their wages and working conditions. Early in the campaign Phil had asked him to join. He had told Phil that he had no use for unions since twice before he had been a member of different unions and "all they ever did for me was to cost me my job and to lose a lot of dues for nothing both times."

He had worked in a unionized glove factory in Saylor before going into the Army in 1941. After the war, he returned to his job expecting to have accumulated seniority for his four and one-half years in service. This would have put him high on the company's seniority list and would have almost guaranteed him what he thought would be reasonable job security. After he had been at work for some three months, he said, he was laid off for no apparent reason while others with less seniority kept their jobs. He complained to the president of the local, but "the union didn't do nothing for me. They just didn't even pay attention to me."

Later he got a job in a small machine shop shortly before it was unionized. In the midst of the organizing campaign, the company closed its doors and the entire work force was locked out. Some months later, five or six workers were rehired, but he was not.

I voted myself right out of a job when I voted for that union. This time I decided to stick with the boss once and see what happens. No union ever done me any good and they cost me a lot. I can't see where they do anything for anybody. If a person don't like his wages or working conditions, why doesn't he go somewhere else? This is a free country, and everybody has the chance of working anywhere he wants to. If you don't like your boss or the wages he pays, go find one that you're satisfied with. America is still a free country and a man has the right to join a union or not. That's his right.

He was critical of many union members whom he knew.

Several of my friends here in town are good union people, so they say, but they hire non-union painters to paint their houses and go down to the scab barber shop in town to save 25 cents on a haircut. I always go to the union barber shop. I don't look for a union label in things that I buy, and when I go to a barber shop, I don't go because it's union or not union. I go there because I want to. But these so-called good union men go to the scab shop to save a few nickels. During the strike one of the strikers whose wife was on strike, too, would drive her to the picket line and then he would take off and work for a non-union painter. I can't see that stuff. What kind of union men are they? If you want to belong to a union, you should belong — but not like that. He stayed out of the union, and shortly after the strike ended he was promoted to the ranks of supervision.

These sketches of the non-joiners are not to be taken as typical, nor can it be assumed that they are atypical. Too few individuals were interviewed to make any definite statement about the behavior of the group. Nevertheless, they do point to the kinds of reasons workers may have for resisting unionism and some social characteristics associated with those reasons. Further, the concentration of non-joiners in two mill departments indicates that they, like the union members, were heavily influenced by their closest co-workers.

The presence of non-joiners among the mill workers was to have profound implications for all concerned. Joining or not joining the union was only the first stage in the developing conflict.

4

Prelude to a Strike

When a union is attempting to organize the workers in a plant, an employer is faced with a limited number of alternatives. He may quietly encourage his employees to join the union; he may adopt a policy of neutrality by not expressing his views one way or the other; or he may oppose the union and make this known to his employees. Which of the courses an employer takes depends on many factors, singly or in combination: previous experience with unions, what he conceives his prerogatives as a manager to be, the way in which he assesses the strength of the union, the possible costs involved in opposing the union, the degree of loyalty to the company which he presumes his employees will maintain, and others.

Tom Miller appeared to view the union as an alien and foreign influence at work in what he considered an otherwise harmonious situation. He felt the union sought to disrupt the relationship between himself and his workers and to wrest from him areas of control which he had always viewed as his own. Accordingly, he chose to oppose the union actively and openly.

Two days after the first open union meeting, he mailed a printed letter to each employee:

Dear Co-Worker:

It appears that a professional labor Promoter is responsible for a campaign designed to "organize" the people working at the Saylor Company.

The law insures every employee the right to join a union if he so desires, and to campaign for a union. The law also insures to every employee the right to refuse to join a union and also gives every employee the right to campaign against unionization if he so desires.

THE MANAGEMENT OF THIS COMPANY DOES NOT WANT A UNION, BECAUSE WE FEEL THAT OUR EMPLOYEES WILL NOT BENEFIT BY BELONGING TO THE UNION. Just why ambitious outsiders have become so interested in "protecting" your rights we do not understand. Perhaps the sizable chunk of money which the union would get from our employees in the form of dues, assessments, etc., is the plum which the union wants to pick.

With the cooperation of our employees and without the interference of any outsiders, we have made the Saylor Company a good place in which to work. Our wages, hours and working conditions compare favorably with those of other plants in this area and with the plants of others with whom we are in competition. You have received the benefits of this high standard without having to pay initiation fees, union dues and various special union assessments. We have undoubtedly made mistakes — who hasn't. Wherever they have been made they have been, and will continue to be, corrected just as soon as they are discovered. No outsider will be required to accomplish this.

What the intervention of these strangers would mean in our relationship, no one can foretell. All of us know that unions engage in business interruptions and strikes and that frequently these cause substantial financial loss to the employees and their families. We, and you, also know that if you are a member of the union you must carry out the commands of the union officials. This frequently requires not only a financial outlay on the part of the member of the union, but picketing and similar outside union activities.

Remember these things:

1. You do not have to join any union to "protect" your jobs.
2. You can refuse to talk to union organizers.
3. You can refuse to sign a membership card. If you have already signed one, you can withdraw from membership in the union by notifying the union.
4. No solicitation is permitted under the Company rules during the working time of either the solicitor or the person being solicited.
5. While we are and will continue to do everything possible to assure you that you will not be subjected to intimidation, coercion or force,

we have learned that at least one employee was told by the organizer that unless she signed the membership card and joined the union now that she would have to join at a later date at a higher cost or she would be one of the first ones laid off of work. WE AGAIN REPEAT THAT YOU DO NOT HAVE TO JOIN ANY UNION TO PROTECT YOUR JOB.

I am advised that our employees have been subjected to a lot of campaign propaganda by these union promoters. I am sure that our people will not be misled by it, and will take what they hear with the proverbial "grain of salt."

The most effective way of meeting this campaign of false promises and misrepresentations is for you, the employees, to step in to see that none of your fellow employees are misled by it. You have just as much of an interest in protecting your fellow employees from this false union propaganda as the Management has — probably more.

I am personally convinced that the intrusion of a union into our relationship here would be bad for both the Company and its employees, and for that reason the union should be opposed by the employees. I hope you will agree with that position.

If you have any questions on this subject, I wish that you would feel free to put them to me and to give me the privilege of answering them. Feel free to write to me or pay me a personal visit in my office which has always been open to you.

      Sincerely,
    s/ T. F. MILLER
      Saylor Company

  The following day, on September 12, the union petitioned the National Labor Relations Board for an election. When the NLRB field examiners arrived in Saylor three days later, Phil privately pointed out to them the importance of an early election because production was at a peak and would begin to drop off in some thirty days. He felt that the company would attempt to delay an election until the slack season when many mill workers were laid off.

  At the same time, Phil was concerned with the impact of Mr. Miller's letter upon the new union members. Helen reported that a few of them were frightened, but that most viewed as a joke the employer's assertions that wages paid in the mill compared favorably with those paid in the area and in the industry. "Some work needs to be done to keep up the interest," she wrote. "I had a few of the girls over to my room after the 10 P.M. shift. I bought some lunch meat and cheese crackers, bread and mustard and had lunch and drink for them. They get a kick out of that."

Two members of the "inside" organizing committee reported that at least some departmental supervisors were actively opposing the union. One supervisor said that the mill workers would be far better off without a union because if they had a union in the plant, they would have to pay dues and assessments, less work would be available, and strikes were possible. "I have the office full of people daily looking for jobs," he added.

To counter the employer's move, Phil addressed a letter to all employees, union and non-union.

You received a letter from the company telling you that it does not want a union. Of course not. A union in the shop means better wages, decent vacations, paid holidays and paid insurance. It means job security and a voice in your everyday life in the shop. The company — just like most companies — does not want you to have it. But 16 million Americans have it and benefit greatly by it. Why shouldn't you?

The letter you received tried to frighten you by referring to initiation fees, assessments and dues. Too bad the company didn't speak to the people in the shop before writing it. They would have learned — as you already know — that you pay no initiation fees, that there never are any assessments and that the dues, which will not be paid until *after* a contract is signed providing for the wages, working conditions and benefits you need and are entitled to, will be collected and controlled by the members from the shop.

The letter warns you against "intimidation, coercion or force." Have you felt or heard anything like that? Why can't the company be decent and honest? Or is it so afraid of having to pay a proper wage?

The letter tried to frighten you with name calling. It says the people from the union which you have met are "professional labor promoters" and "ambitious strangers." It is sad that any company will use such tactics. Perhaps if they had taken the trouble to meet these people or to speak to you about them, the company would have known better than to use words like that.

The company is trying to frighten you with the word "strike" just as Russia is trying to frighten our country with the word "war." The workers at the mill are not frightened by the words in the letter you received any more than free Americans are frightened by Russia.

The letter is accurate in one respect. It states: *"The law insures every employee the right to join a union if he so desires and to campaign for a union."* That is true. The election by secret ballot which will soon be held will prove to the company that the workers know they are protected by the law and the union and that they want a union and a union contract.

We have said and say again that it is the desire of the workers and the officers of the union to help the company run its business successfully. But we insist on the right to a union contract with wages and working conditions comparable to those of other organized workers in the country.

It's about time that T. Miller stopped listening to his high powered supervisors who are afraid for their petty powers and started listening to the workers in the shop and to their needs.

Fraternally yours,
s/ PHILIP G. DRAPER

At the same time Phil urged Helen to spend the major portion of her time seeing the "key people" — the "inside" organizing committee — to strengthen their convictions and to emphasize the need for solidarity in the face of the company's attack. Phil again wrote to Mr. Miller, claiming that 172 of the workers had now signed union membership cards and asking that the company either recognize the union or consent to an early election. The company responded by engaging a firm of Milwaukee attorneys to represent their interests. The attorneys notified Phil that the company refused to recognize the union, refused to consent to an election, and insisted that the NLRB would have to hold hearings on the union's demand for an election.

Three days later, a "captive audience"[1] meeting of all mill workers was held in the plant cafeteria. Mr. Miller stated clearly that he was opposed to the union. He told the workers that unions often made such excessive demands that companies were forced out of business. He had planned a month before to raise wages, he said, but now that the union was a factor in the situation, he could not do it because the union might bring an unfair labor practice charge before the National Labor Relations Board. He urged the union members to withdraw by writing to the regional office of the union, and he encouraged all employees to come to him with any problems. He expressed confi-

---

[1] This term refers to a plant meeting called by an employer during working hours which all workers are required to attend.

dence that the workers would "know how to vote" in the coming Labor Board election.

When this meeting was reported to the organizers, they were convinced that the employer was about to embark on an all-out counter-offensive. With this in mind, Phil sent another letter to all employees.

As we thought might happen, the Company held a meeting in the shop. We hope the Company will have the decency to pay you for the time you were forced to lose from your piecework jobs.

Most of the threats and insinuations made are too silly to answer. But two statements made by the Company have to be nailed down.

You were told that the National Labor Relations Board is trying to decide whether or not an election should be held. This is not true. You have the legal right to hold an election and one will be held in the very near future. The Company is trying to delay an election hoping that it can talk you out of a Union contract which will give you better wages and working conditions. But the law is on our side and the Company will not succeed.

You were also told that the Company intended to give raises in August but it cannot do it now because of the Union. What an excuse! And isn't it strange that the Company didn't think about raises until the Union was started. The Company knows now that increased wages will be put into Union contracts where they'll stick — and which cannot be taken away later.

All this fancy maneuvering on the part of the Company will soon stop — the election will be won — a Union contract signed.

In the meantime, don't let the Company fool you.

Both Phil and Helen were confident that if an election were held immediately, the union would win an overwhelming majority. They also were convinced that the company was trying to delay the election in the hope that in the interim it would destroy the union. Therefore, it was even more important for them to build and maintain as strong a union group as possible.

Helen began holding daily departmental meetings in her hotel room. Her goal was to involve all of the union members in the developing struggle and to strengthen her contact system so that the union could communicate quickly with workers inside the mill. But she was increasingly concerned at the delay in holding the representation election. She reported to Phil that "everyone is so unsettled in the shop and raising hell with me. . . . The men have been very patient and understanding, but now even they are grumbling." A few days later, the company dealt the union a severe blow. Two workers went through the plant circulating petitions notifying the union officials that the signers had withdrawn their membership. In all, about twenty-five workers signed their names.

Phil decided that the time had come to enlist some help from other unions in Saylor. He explained the situation to officials of the Trades and Labor Council, who promised that they would initiate a movement to inform their members of Mr. Miller's opposition tactics and to ask them to "spread it around town."

In the meantime Helen invited those workers who had signed the petitions to meet in her room. She told the dozen who came that the company had circulated the petitions to find out which workers were union members and that now it was all the more important for the union to win the election since only the union could protect their jobs.

At this point, Phil addressed another letter to each member.

The Company got two of the workers to pass petitions through the shop asking you to withdraw from the Union. There are always one or two in every large group who are willing to sell themselves to the boss cheaply and in return for his favor are willing to hurt their fellow workers.

The Company never knew who did or did not sign a Union card. By signing these petitions that are being circulated, those few who signed them were letting the Company know for the first time that they had signed Union cards. That was not a wise thing to do.

The organizing campaign is coming to a close. Ninety per cent of the workers have joined the union and the election is not too far off. The statements made to you by Union representatives are as true today as they were when they first talked to you. Neither you nor any other workers in the shop can possibly be hurt by signing a Union card and having a Union in your shop. The Federal law protects you in this respect as it does all other workers in the country.

But you do have very much to lose if the Company succeeds in frightening you away from your original intentions of having a Union. The Company will then feel justified not only in keeping wages down but in cutting them whenever it likes.

This is the best chance that you ever had to bring a Union into your shop and a Union contract into effect which will give you a decent wage instead of a petty increase and the false promises that you had for these many years that the shop was in existence.

Do not be deceived by traitors in your ranks. It means nothing if you were frightened by them into signing these petitions. You are still a member and you can still vote for the Union. Stick by your co-workers and insist upon a Union contract and all the good that a Union contract can do for you.

On October 10, when the union and the company received the news that the Labor Board had scheduled the representation election for October 24, both the union and company intensified their campaigns for the allegiance of the workers. The company sent a letter to all employees stating that "this vicious union drive . . . is practically turning the peaceful atmosphere of our plant and our relations with our employees, into what looks like to us guerrilla warfare," and that the "professional union organizers" were spreading lies.

These professional union organizers . . . are constantly trying, through every means at their hand, through lies and continually badgering and bothering you in what we believe is a vain attempt to win this election.

. . . It is our purpose to free you as fast as possible from this disorder which the union organizers have created here, so that you may again live in peace amongst yourselves and with us. . . .

We understand also that these people are making the most extravagant promises to you as to what they are going to do for you. You have no guarantee, of course, that these promises will be fulfilled. From what we hear, they are just dreams. You can rest assured that a union is not necessary to get you anything that is possible for us to give. We will do that ourselves pleasantly and decently, without any disturbances and strife, such as you have here at the present time.

As against this turmoil which now exists, we have had peace in this plant ever since we have been in business. We have had no disorders, no strikes, and no picketing. From the manner in which these union organizers are conducting this union drive, it is hard to say what may happen if the union comes in here. But, what we do know is that the history of unionism is full of cases where when the union becomes the bargaining agent, the most peaceful and pleasant relationship between employees and employers is disturbed, sometimes so seriously that those conditions never become right again. Whether this would happen here, no one can foretell. But, we ask you — Do you think the risk is worth while?

Phil scheduled a meeting at the Trades Council hall on the following Saturday. The publicity leaflet urged "everyone — those for and those against a Union . . . to exercise your rights as a citizen in a free country" by coming to the meeting. At the meeting Phil discussed the company's latest attack on the union — the contention that the company would give the employees everything possible without a union. He pointed out that the company actually was paying its employees only what the federal minimum wage law required — 75 cents an hour — while other workers in the area and in the industry earned much more than that. He maintained that the company was acting like a "spoiled child who cannot have its way and now starts calling names. The company cries that the peaceful atmosphere of the plant is gone." The representation election, he stated, would give the workers the opportunity "to tell the company that you want a peaceful atmosphere, but that you also want a union contract with better wages, job security, and union benefits." How the workers voted would determine whether the company would continue to pay and do what it wanted or whether the workers would have a voice in the conditions of their employment. He concluded by saying that the company had failed its employees and it was time for a change.

A pre-election rally was scheduled for the Saturday afternoon preceding the election. The Midwest general organizer of the union and his chief assistant came from Chicago to be featured speakers, and the president of the Saylor Trades and Labor Council also was on the program. The speakers outlined the union's demands: (1) union recognition, (2) substantial raises for all job classifications, (3) company-paid insurance and retirement fund, (4) orderly grievance procedure, (5) no cuts in piece rates after they were set.

The organizers sympathized with the Saylor Company mill workers because their piecework rates were so low that they could earn no more than the guaranteed minimum, and they emphasized that both minimum rates and piecework earnings in shops organized by the union were, on the average, 15 cents an hour higher. They added that premium bonus rates for production over the guaranteed minimum also were higher in organized shops. Saylor workers were told that they, in contrast, were getting a bonus for not making the minimum rate and that this was not a bonus at all. Further, because there was no way for the employees to determine whether or not the company-set piecework prices were fair, workers on a given operation might be paid 10 cents a dozen one season and only a third as much the next time for the same operation.

The speakers took exception to the mill's "grab bag system" of distributing work: those workers who arrived first at the beginning of each shift were allowed to pick the easiest and/or highest paying work. They also criticized the servicing of operators: because they usually had to leave their machines to get materials, their output and earnings were decreased substantially. In addition, they said, many of these workers found that they had to do a great deal of extra work on some items, and no allowance was made for the extra work.

"Maybe you're satisfied with these conditions," Phil said. "The company thinks so. They promise that without the union you can get along as well as before." The speakers joined in urging the workers to take the first step toward correcting the bad conditions in the mill by voting for the union in the coming election. Leaflets containing the substance of the talks were distributed as the meeting closed.

Another union leaflet was distributed at the mill gates the day before the election. Under the heading, "The Union Wants Peace in the Mill," it set forth the general demands for wage increases, an end to favoritism in the mill, vacations, health and retirement plans, and an equitable piecework system.

In the meantime, the mill superintendent was conducting "captive audience" meetings in the mill cafeteria. Workers were told of the strikes in which unions engage, of the cost of some of these strikes in terms of lost wages and permanent loss of jobs when a struck employer lost customers because he was unable to fulfill delivery commitments. Tom Miller, speaking at one of these meetings, said in effect that a nearby competitor had been driven out of business because of excessive demands made by the same union organizers at work in Saylor.

As it happened, one of the members of the "inside" organizing committee had a friend who was employed at the competing factory. She wrote to her, asking for more information about the situation there. The friend responded that the factory had been sold some three years after the union was organized and that the new owner had temporarily discontinued the operation because it interfered with clock manufacturing going on in the same building. However, the company later re-established the discontinued product. The friend reported wage levels in her unionized factory, and they turned out to be substantially higher than those in the Saylor mill. This letter was circulated by the "inside" organizing committee and appeared to spike the employer's claims effectively.

On the day of the representation election, the union distributed a leaflet to employees going into the mill to work and to vote. The leaflet, which became the basis for a seven months' delay in the final certification of election results, is quoted in full:

What is the History of the Right to Organize?

Everyone knows that, from the beginning of our industrial history, employers almost without exception have fought organization of their workers at every turn. What is organization for? It is to give each worker the strength and protection of united effort. It is to clothe the nakedness of the unorganized worker who is otherwise forced to stand single handed and alone. No bona-fide unions, free from company domination and Russian domination, want trouble. THE RIGHT TO ORGANIZE COMES FROM ALMIGHTY GOD HIMSELF.

CATHOLIC BISHOP FRANCIS J. HAAS
GRAND RAPIDS, MICHIGAN

P.S. . . . DON'T BE FOOLED BY COMPANY PROPAGANDA.

In the election, 116 of 216 eligible mill employees voted to have the union represent them for the purposes of collective bargaining. The results made it clear that the company's counteroffensive had been more successful than the organizers had assessed. Whereas approximately 80 per cent of the workers had signed union membership cards up to the two-week period prior to the election, only 57 per cent voted for the union in the secret election.

The company's strategy now was to try to delay certification of the union as sole bargaining agency in the hope that the election could be set aside and that a new election might result in the union's defeat. Two days after the election, the company's attorneys filed objections with the NLRB regional office. The objections were based on two allegations: (1) the union leaflet quoting Bishop Haas consisted of undue and illegal pressure, and (2) the leaflet was distributed at the polling places in violation of the Board rule that no electioneering should take place within thirty feet of the polls.

Again the union representatives addressed a letter to all members stating that no matter what new "tricks" the company devised, the union would not be stopped.

The Company told you it wanted a democratic election. It didn't mean it! The Company thought it had enough of you frightened so that you would vote the way it wanted. But when the election was held, a majority voted against the Company and for a Union.

The Company then forgot about democracy and decided to use legal tricks to delay negotiating a Union contract with Union wages and conditions. The Company's tricks failed before and will fail again. The Union and the Federal National Labor Relations Board will take care of these stalling tactics in the near future.

Helen stepped up the meetings of the organizing committee "to keep morale up, but," she wrote, "I'm at a loss as to what to tell them. The people are awaiting the Board's decision impatiently." Union lapel pins were distributed in an effort to bolster waning morale, but members of the "inside" committee reported that very few workers were wearing them and most of the others probably would not until after the final certification of the union. Inside leaders reported to Helen that the mill superintendent was discriminating against the union members by giving them "bad work." Sue reported, "Morale is very low in the shop, and production is falling off. On top of all this, some new girls were hired in one department taking work away from some of our strong members there."

At the membership meeting on December 7, Phil told the workers that the company was using every means to "stall and delay" negotiating a contract in the hope that it could kill off the union. The organizers realized that the longer certification was delayed, the greater was the possibility of further defections from the union ranks and the greater the problem of maintaining morale among the union members. For the first time Phil suggested that strike action might be necessary.

The next day he contacted a union official in the headquarters city of the NLRB regional office and asked help in getting a quick Board ruling on the company's appeal. The Regional Director denied the company's objections on December 19. A week later the company appealed, this time by filing exceptions to the regional director's report with the NLRB in Washington. At the same time, the company confronted the union with another dilemma. It announced a general 15-cent wage increase for all employees.

Phil was faced with an important problem: could the union find a way to turn this latest company move to its own advantage? The union could file charges with the NLRB that the unilateral wage increase amounted to an unfair labor practice under the Taft-Hartley Act — refusal to bargain. But this move might give the workers the impression that the union opposed the increase, and Phil wanted to avoid this interpretation. Also, involving the Labor Board further in the case would result in more delay in certification of the union and negotiation of a contract. The whole campaign would then be more difficult for the union.

Phil decided on another tactic. He wrote a letter to all employees, arguing that the raise was given only in the hope that the union could be weakened, and asserting that without a union contract, any raises given by the company could be taken away just as easily. He pointed out that the raise was given only because of the threat of the union, and that if only the threat could produce results, the union itself could do much more for the workers. He stated that the company was spending "a fortune" on attorneys who had been hired to think up "tricks" to stop the union, and added that it would have been much wiser for the company to pay that money to the workers. He also asked everyone to come to a general membership meeting the following evening:

I said at that meeting the Company gave them a raise simply because of the pressure brought on them by the union. I said that we could file charges with the Labor Board against them and if we won, the raise would be taken away but that's not what we're here for. They got the raise — swell, that's the first installment, and we'll go out for more.

The way in which the increase was applied convinced Phil that neither the employer nor his attorneys understood the rationale of the firm's own piecework system. In general, the system is based on the premise that workers will increase their output if a bonus is paid for extra work. But when a worker is guaranteed an amount of pay which is close to or equal to what he formerly earned including a bonus, he no longer has an incentive to do any extra work.

The minimum hourly guaranteed rates at the Saylor mill had doubled over a three-year period, but piecework bonus prices had not changed. Thus the incentives had been constantly diluted until they had all but disappeared. The latest increase in the guaranteed minimum from 75 to 90 cents actually worked to the disadvantage of both the employees and the company since it almost destroyed the incentive; when workers found it difficult to achieve the output on which the minimum guarantee was based, they were reprimanded by their supervisors for not "making out." Phil summed up the situation:

The Company used very smart lawyers insofar as the use of the Taft-Hartley Act was concerned. But they used very stupid lawyers insofar as the industry was concerned. They knew nothing of the industry and apparently the Company knew very little of the methods of wage payment. The increase they gave was put on the wrong end. What was logical from the factory point of view — not necessarily the union's — was to provide increases in the piece rate prices to give an incentive so that the people would turn out more than the 75 cents an hour they were already guaranteed. What they did in this situation was to actually cut down the incentive. The whole thing didn't avail the Company anything. The people were just as intent immediately after the raise as they were immediately prior to the raise to keep on going with the union.

It was not necessary for him to point out to the affected workers that the new increase actually created a new inequity.

That particular part was brought to my attention in an awful hurry by the people who were already aware of it. Because by that time, there had been enough discussion among the people in the shop about piece rate prices and incentives in a piecework shop so that the people understood it. In fact, it seemed to me that they understood it better than Tom Miller did. And when the raise was announced, the people called it to my attention. I did point out that our need was no longer to increase the minimum but to try to bring the necessary results to both the workers and the Company. And the people pointed out to me — a lot of them said: "What the hell is the use of working if I can't possibly make that much money anyway!" There must be some differential between a minimum and the incentive — otherwise the shop goes to hell.

It now seemed to Phil that the struggle for a union contract would probably be won only through strike action. Yet both he and Helen were extremely reluctant to urge this course since they were not at all certain that the membership was ready to follow a strike recommendation. First they had to strengthen the organization. Phil wrote to the "inside" organizing committee that "the fact that the Company is so anxious to avoid a Union contract should make the people in the shop all the more interested in a contract." Anything the company wants so desperately to do without, he said, must be very precious and important to the workers.

More than ever before, all of us will have to strive to make this understandable to the workers in the shop, to bolster up their spirits and to make them be willing not only to wait but to fight, if necessary.

Phil sent a second full-time organizer to Saylor to help prepare for a possible strike. Chuck, who was in his early thirties, had been a skilled worker in a Milwaukee plant organized by Phil and an officer of his local union before joining Phil's staff. He had had several years' experience in organizing and had been through several strikes. His assignment was to aid Helen in maintaining the morale of the group and to lay whatever groundwork was necessary in preparation for a strike.

Chuck met the "inside" committee in his hotel room and suggested that a strike might be the only way out. He told the members he wanted their reactions to this suggestion and urged that they discuss it with the people in the mill. His report to Phil on this meeting stated: "Half are eager and the remainder are those who think a little more of the consequences of a strike." Two weeks later, Chuck reported, "The story that a strike is possible if the Company keeps up its present tactics has penetrated to all corners of the shop, and it seems that it is talked about by everybody." Yet the organizers could not assess the feelings of the workers toward a strike because sentiment had not crystallized. This was a new and as yet undefined experience for the Saylor people. The organizers felt that it was necessary to build the strongest possible sentiment for a strike before it was undertaken. Further, the company's appeal to the NLRB was still pending, and the union was determined to "play the string out as far as it goes."

On February 20, almost four months after the election was held, the national Board confirmed the Regional Director's certification of the union, when it held that the leaflet distributed at the polling places fell within the realm of legitimate election propaganda and that there was no evidence of electioneering within thirty feet of the polls. The following day Phil wired the employer requesting that a date be set immediately to begin contract negotiations. A week later, the company's attorneys replied that the company was filing a motion with the NLRB, asking it to reconsider its decision.

The company now repeated a tactic which had been somewhat successful earlier. Mr. Miller addressed all workers in the company cafeteria and urged them to write to the regional office of the union asking that their names be dropped from the list of union members. During this meeting he again hinted that other firms had either closed or moved to other towns after their work forces had been unionized. He did not state that this would happen in his case, but the impression he left seemed clear. In a community where very few or no alternative opportunities for employment existed, such inferences may carry great weight among employees. The union received sixteen letters notifying the union officials that the senders (in each instance individuals who had once before withdrawn membership by signing petitions) had withdrawn. Since the union had won the certification election with a scant 57 per cent majority, the new defections were viewed as serious.

Helen and Chuck visited each of the defectors as well as others who had signed the petition of withdrawal the previous October. The "inside" committee also contacted as many of them as possible in an effort to bring them back into the union's ranks. The union representatives were less than successful. They reported very little progress, but some hope since "the non-union people don't seem to be anti-union. They're just waiting for some sign from us of real progress before they jump on the bandwagon." Helen added that she was using a different tactic with these workers who were now referred to as "fence-sitters":

I just call and tell them I am very surprised about their withdrawal and just wanted to talk to them, not to ask them to re-sign but to let them know what is happening. Of course I tell them I don't want them to be hurt because I've taken a personal liking to them, and when we have a strike here the fact that they are not union members, they will not be able to draw strike benefits while the union members will be taken care of. I leave without saying anything about re-signing, and I only ask them to think things over and if they want to talk to me, I will be at the hotel or I will gladly arrange to return to see them.

Chuck also emphasized that strike benefits would be paid only to union members. The "inside" committee reported to Helen that "they are talking strike throughout the shop." Phil and Helen were convinced that if the committee continued to talk about a strike, there was some chance that the defectors would rejoin. This, however, did not come about.

Helen met with leaders of the Trades and Labor Council to solicit their help in spreading the word around town that there might be a strike and that "if the girls go on the picket line at the factory, the Trades and Labor Council will be back of them and start boycotting the store because Miller is unfair to labor." The Council leaders agreed to ask their memberships for support. Phil urged Bert (now president of the mill local) to tell the people in the shop that "the Company will have to do business with us or the International Union will have to recommend to the people in the shop to go out on strike." He wanted Bert to make sure that "everyone understands fully the sort of Company that they have to deal with." At the same time, Phil wrote to Helen:

We have not as yet reached a stage where we want to issue statements to the press or to hold any mass meetings in which to arouse the sentiments of the people both in the shop and in the community. But that step may be reached in a short time. You have been through this before and know what I mean. More than ever before, we need an aroused group in the shop.

The latest company appeal to the NLRB made it difficult for Phil to pace the strike agitation. It was the international union's policy to wait for a decision on a company's final legal resort before recommending a strike, but Phil had no way of knowing when that decision might come — how many days, weeks, or months hence. He asked the international union's general counsel in New York to do what he could to expedite the Board's decision.

The union officials, however, miscalculated the effects of the strike agitation upon the local leadership. The union policy of permitting the company to exhaust its recourse before the Labor Board was interpreted by several of the local leaders as an unnecessary delay in calling a strike. They had become convinced that only a successful strike would force the company to come to terms and that the union was responsible for delaying the showdown. One leader charged Phil with "letting grass grow under your feet. . . . The girls at the mill are all disgusted, and if you don't get going, the union will fold like a tent. . . ." Helen reported that other leaders were asking, "How much longer is Phil going to let this go on? We are beginning to believe the union is going to let the damn thing go until we lose everything. . . . Phil is stalling." The chief organizer commented:

On the part of some people, there was a feeling of frustration and the desire to start screaming or go on strike to overcome this frustration. . . . Nothing seemed to be happening . . . we weren't much closer to a contract. They started thinking — "Well, the Company was right in the first instance — that Tom Miller and the Miller family was much too big for any union to come in and set themselves up, and that despite everything Phil had said to us, there will never be a union here. Tom Miller won again."

Phil assured the leaders by letter, by telephone, and in person that the union was doing everything in its power to avoid delays and to secure a contract. He pointed out that the union already had invested a tremendous amount of time, effort, and money to build their union. He argued that the company was responsible for the long delays and that it was necessary for the leaders to "get the people to understand the Company's delaying tactics and build up sentiments for a strike. If and when that time comes, we want to be sure that we have a large percentage of the people on the picket line and not inside the shop working." He said that the simplest course of action would be to call an immediate strike. "But it has been and continues to be the policy of our union to take every possible step before we ask our members to go on strike." Should strike action become necessary, he wrote, adequate preparation must come first.

A responsible union does not go into a strike haphazardly any more than a country goes into a war haphazardly. . . . We will choose a time when the company's business is expanding and it will hurt the most. We will also want to be sure that we have a substantial number of people who will go on strike so that we have reason to expect a quick victory. When we do recommend a strike, we will do so because we are certain that there is no possibility of getting a contract any other way.

Although Phil emphasized the strike policy of the international union in his talks and letters, his real reservation stemmed from the fact that only a very slim majority of workers stood openly for the union. He could not be sure that the majority in the shop would respect picket lines in case of a strike. He felt that the new union members still identified themselves closely with the employer — but to confess this to the local leadership would be to increase their apprehensions and to decrease their confidence in him.

Several of the local union leaders continued to blame the union for not forcing the issue, while others tended to blame the employer's attorneys. Very few felt that Mr. Miller himself held the key to the situation. The organizers continually pointed out to the local leadership that

attorneys don't do things on their own but do things under instructions from their clients. The turning point would be reached when the people understood this. It was a question of them understanding that if Miller wanted, all this would be unnecessary. It was necessary for them to understand that if Miller intended a fair compromise with the union, there would be no need for a strike or the continuance of a strike once it started.

On March 28, 1951, seven months after the election, the National Labor Relations Board denied the company's motion for reconsideration of its earlier decision. The company's recourse under the law was now exhausted. The first meeting between the employer and his representatives and the union representatives for the purpose of negotiating a contract was held April 6 in Saylor. In eight negotiating sessions during the course of the next three months, some progress was made on issues which the union considered relatively unimportant: the mechanics of the grievance procedure, the union's right to review piecework prices, improved methods for supplying workers with materials, a job classification system which would rationalize the wage structure materially, and others. However, no agreement was reached on two issues which the union leaders considered vital: union security and an across-the-board wage increase.

On June 14. Helen reported to Phil that "the workers are getting very restless — they want action. So we started a rumor that Miller was going to cut wages back to 75 cents an hour." The results far exceeded her expectations: "There is so much strike talk in the mill that the Company is working everyone at full speed — at least eight hours and some departments on Saturday. Everyone is sure that without a union they will surely face a wage-cut." She went on to report that supervisors were quietly advising non-members that they would lose their jobs if they joined the union, but that workers in the inspection department had told a forelady to "get the hell out of here before we throw you out . . ." when she suggested that the union was not really interested in the workers' welfare.

Several of the skilled craftsmen, the prestige group among the mill workers, also began making house calls to let the non-members know that they were prepared to strike for the union demands. During the negotiating session on June 29, the company's attorney insisted that some union representatives "were, in effect, badgering the employees who were not members of the union to force them to become members." Union representatives replied that such actions, if they were taking place, were without the knowledge or consent of the union. Mr. Miller stated that if the "badgering" continued, he would be forced to take disciplinary action against any union members "using this type of solicitation" or to discharge the guilty people.

The company broke off negotiations at this meeting, and both sides agreed to request assistance from the Federal Mediation and Conciliation Service. Several meetings with the conciliator spread over most of a week failed to produce a basis upon which the union representatives felt they could agree with the company. The company was willing to grant five paid holidays, some individual adjustments in piece rates, a grievance procedure, and other provisions but did not yield on the two issues which the union considered vital — the union security clause and the across-the-board wage increase. Without these concessions, the other items, when totaled by the union, did not amount to much. The company's final offer, said Phil, "would be considered a defeat by the people in the shop for all their efforts and their time." The success of the company in cutting the union's majority in the plant to what was almost a minority convinced Phil that only with a union shop could the local hope to continue in business for a year, during which time it could repair its forces and prepare for contract improvements the following year.

A complete impasse was reached late in the afternoon of the second day of almost continuous negotiations. Each side stood at fixed and deadlocked positions with the union shop and wage issues unresolved. At this point the conciliator suggested that the issues be submitted to arbitration. The union negotiators agreed to the proposal but the employer took the position that no "outsider" would be permitted to decide how the mill should be run. The union committee, now convinced that further discussion was not likely to be at all fruitful, asked for a recess and decided that there was no alternative to a strike.

Before the local could act, Phil had to call the union regional vice-president in Chicago to secure permission. Permission was granted, and the negotiating committee was sent to the mill gates at shift change to tell members of the "inside" organizing committee (by this time about twenty workers) to come immediately to a meeting in Phil's hotel room.

Phil explained the situation and recommended that the union call a strike the next day. When the committee supported the recommendation unanimously, Phil moved to call a general membership meeting for a strike vote. Since there was no time to distribute leaflets, each committee member was given a block of names and telephone numbers of union members and instructed to notify them of the special meeting that evening at the local Trades and Labor hall.

Approximately 125 mill workers were present when Phil dispassionately reported on the conduct of negotiation and the final company offer. The union's attorney spoke in detail on the company's position and how the union interpreted it. Phil again took the floor to announce that the international union was recommending a strike. He listed what he considered to be the alternatives: accept the company's final offer which probably would result in the disappearance of the union, abandon the entire effort, or force the issue through a strike. The union had been very patient, he said; it had not taken this step until all legal procedures had been exhausted. It had given the firm every opportunity to come to a fair agreement with the union. But he insisted that any agreement had to include a union security clause, because unless the union had this protection, the company would never cease trying to destroy it. Further, any agreement had to include a "decent" wage increase. Since the company was unwilling to concede these issues through discussion, a strike was the only alternative. He promised that the strike would be fully supported by the resources of an international union with more than 400,000 members. The local union president made a short speech in support of Phil's strike motion. He was convinced, he said, that only a strike could show Tom Miller that the union members were absolutely determined to get a "decent" contract. He told the meeting that the bargaining committee stood "100 per cent" behind Phil and the strike move and that, although they had all hoped that this action might be avoided, they were unanimous in the belief that there was now no other recourse.

A short discussion period followed. Someone asked if any strike benefits would be paid. Phil replied that it was the policy of the international to pay benefits to strikers and to make sure that no one suffered "undue hardship." He again emphasized the resources of the union, trying to assure those present that the union "would take care of them." Someone else asked if they would have to picket and Phil replied that all strikers would be asked to picket but those who felt that they could not would be given other tasks to do such as running the strike headquarters and the kitchen which would be set up. The discussion continued for about thirty minutes after which the motion to strike was put to a standing vote. About 115 of the 125 present stood for the organizer's motion. The strike was on.

5

The Strike

Shortly before 6 o'clock on the morning of July 12, a picket line formed at the main entrance of the Saylor Company. Although more than a hundred employees had voted to strike the previous night, the line consisted of exactly two persons — Phil and Helen. Small groups of union members gathered across the street from the mill entrance, awaiting directions from their leaders. Only a handful had any notion of what a picket was supposed to do. The rest had never before acted on a strike stage.

Because the strike had been called in a hurry, there had been no time to organize picket teams, appoint picket captains, secure necessary placards, or assign pickets to the different mill entrances, driveways, and loading dock. Yet the organizers anticipated that any sort of a picket line would serve as a deterrent if the employer should attempt to continue production and employees who were not union members should attempt to enter the plant.

The mill itself stretched over almost half a city block with one side facing an alley and the other three facing city streets. The alley separated the mill from a parking lot which occupied the remainder of the block. About sixty of the workers standing across the street volunteered for picket duty, but Phil had to know precisely where the company property was located before he could assign them. Three city policemen who appeared on the scene told him that the entire block was Miller property. Phil decided that his small force could not possibly cover the whole area and that the immediate need was to place pickets at the four mill entrances, the loading dock, and the rear entrance facing the alley. However, he could see no way to block attempts to enter the mill from the alley.

It quickly became evident, as the organizers had anticipated, that at least some employees did want to work. The pickets had been hastily instructed to stop such attempts, but at this point they did not consider physical resistance as proper. As small groups of non-members approached the plant entrances, the strikers confronted them and tried to talk them out of going in. Sometimes simple conversation was enough. When discussion failed, the pickets would shout for Phil or Helen or one of the few experienced pickets to come and help. Sometimes they succeeded, but most often they failed. Phil was kept extremely busy rushing from one plant entrance to another, trying to keep people away from their jobs and, at the same time, trying to organize an orderly picket line and to assign specific people to definite picketing tasks.

Many other arrangements had to be made. The force of professional organizers had to be augmented. Arrangements had to be made with the union's Midwest officials for financing the strike. Strike benefits had to be paid. A union kitchen had to be set up and staffed for serving three meals a day to the strikers and their families. A strike headquarters near the plant had to be rented. Arrangements had to be made with the union's international headquarters for bail bond in case any of the union people were arrested. News releases and pickets' placards had to be prepared. All of these matters required Phil's immediate attention.

Phil spent much of the first morning of the strike away from the picket line making these arrangements by telephone and telegraph. One time when he returned to the strike scene he saw a police officer across the street talking to four women workers who were not union members. The officer escorted the women to the picket line in front of the mill's main entrance and told Phil that he was going to take them through and into the plant.

He told me that he has orders that I'm supposed to open up, and I told him his job was to see that everything was run peacefully but not to take scabs through the picket line and that we wouldn't permit it. Then he pushed his weight around a little bit, but it didn't do any good.

Shortly after this, the Mayor of Saylor, the Chief of Police, and twelve or thirteen of the city's seventeen-man force appeared on the scene. Phil attempted to explain privately to the Mayor the union's position with regard to the picket line and the non-strikers. He was unsuccessful. Instead, the Mayor addressed some general remarks to the crowd, saying that it was his "duty to enforce the law and preserve order." What happened next is related by Phil:

The Mayor decided that he wasn't going to listen to anyone, and he and the Chief with the other coppers back of them formed a wedge. They tried to get the people to disperse, and at my suggestion, they didn't. And then they formed a flying wedge and tried going through with the scabs in the center of the wedge. They kicked and pushed their way through the picket line. At this time we had about twenty-five or thirty girls on the line, and I think there were maybe four or five men including myself. It was nothing serious, but there were a number of bruises that turned up a week later on the arms and legs of the women. At first the people on the line didn't know what to do, but when they saw what happened, they became very determined that the Mayor and the cops weren't going to break through. And so they held the line, and then the cops pushed them aside and they went back and formed a new line in back so they were about four or five deep and all across the entrance. And then there was a skirmish — I don't know how long it lasted, but I imagine it didn't last more than a minute, and they held the line and they were screaming at the cops and the Mayor, and Helen was leading the way and screaming at the cops, and then the cops must have realized that they couldn't break through unless they wanted to cause some real physical damage. Even though they seemed determined enough to get the scabs in and bust up the line, they stopped and went away because they didn't have the courage to cause real physical harm to those women.

The Mayor confirmed in substance this account of the incident. A police officer had telephoned him to say that pickets were stopping workers from entering the mill. During the phone conversation, Tom Miller got on the line and confirmed the policeman's report. The Mayor continued his account:

After this telephone call, I went out there with some of the police force, and I told those people who were picketing that anybody who wanted to work had a right, under the law, to do so. It was my duty as Mayor to see that law and order were kept. It was incumbent upon me as Mayor to get the police out there and to see that those who wanted to work were permitted to do so. The maintenance of law and order and the preservation of the peace is my responsibility under local and state statutes. I saw one striker grab a woman by the arm as she tried to go into the place and hold her back. That was enough for me. Four of the women wanted to go in, and I told the pickets that they better open up and let them in or there would be trouble. But that Draper kept running up and down the picket line yelling, "Hold the line — don't let them in!" He got those women out there all excited and I thought what the hell was the use of trying to take those four women in — it would only stir them up more.

At this point the two accounts depart slightly. The Mayor related that the pickets permitted him to enter the plant to discuss the situation with the employer.

They opened the line and let me through. I told Tom Miller that he should close the place up tight — don't try to run it until the strike was settled. I told him that he and his family were living in the horse and buggy days. Labor is here to stay, and they might as well realize that. I told him that if General Motors and the Ford Company gave in to unions, who the hell did he think they were that they could break a union with a little dinky company like that. Especially this union. But those Millers are proud and stubborn people.

Later that morning he spoke in private with the union's chief organizer.

I told that Draper that if he would stop getting those people so riled up and keep them quiet, I'd take the police out of there. But he wouldn't do it. He just kept running around getting people more and more excited. I could have picked him up and that woman organizer he had down there and thrown them in jail for a spell. But that would have only added fuel to the fire and then what would I have on my hands?

Phil was a bit disappointed at the Mayor's refusal to arrest him.

I was trying to get myself picked up. I wanted either one of the organizers or myself to be arrested. You know the old story — the martyr gag. We knew that nothing would happen, but our people didn't. We wanted them to see that in a strike it was possible to get arrested and that it doesn't hurt and not to be afraid. But they wouldn't pick us up. I did everything I could to get them to arrest me, anything that wasn't completely illegal.

Although Phil's desire remained frustrated, he assessed the incident as extremely valuable to the union:

From that moment on, the people knew that a picket sometimes has to fight — they just don't always simply walk a line. And the Mayor did us a tremendous favor. From then on the people were all ready. The feeling was that if they could stop the Mayor, then they could stop anybody from coming in. That educated them as much or more than anything else.

The Mayor was indeed stopped and did not attempt to cross the picket line again. But others were not stopped.

Throughout the remainder of the first day, Phil took care of the many necessary details. The national headquarters of the union arranged with a Saylor insurance firm to provide up to $10,000 bail bond in cases of arrest. The international's regional vice-president approved strike benefits of $10.00 a week for women and $16.00 for men, the difference based on the assumption that women had working husbands. Further, both men and women were given an additional $2.00 for each dependent. Strike duty was to begin at 6 o'clock in the morning, Monday through Friday, and all members who spent at least four hours a day on strike duty were eligible for benefits.

An empty store about two blocks from the mill was rented as a combination strike headquarters and kitchen-dining room. Cooking facilities, tables, and chairs were hastily installed. All workers were asked to picket, but those who felt they could not were assigned to help in the kitchen. A few fence-sitters did daily turns on the picket line, but most of them elected to work in the kitchen. Two additional organizers were sent in from the Chicago regional office, and Chuck, who had been sent out from the state office on a temporary basis, was now assigned to Saylor for the duration of the strike. A local sign painter prepared appropriate picket signs. The "inside" committee was transformed into a strike committee.

HARASSMENT AND VIOLENCE

During the second day of the strike, the city police made the first of a series of arrests. A picket was charged with assault when she attempted to stop a non-striker from entering the plant. The local newspaper reported the incident on its front page:

A woman picket was accused of assault and battery today in the two-day old strike at the Saylor Company. Mrs. Helen Dobbs was accused of scuffling with Mrs. Esther Blaine who was trying to enter the strike-bound plant earlier today. Philip Draper, . . . International Representative for the union, posted $100 bond for Mrs. Dobbs in Police Judge Dan Cowen's court this morning.

Draper pleaded not guilty on behalf of Mrs. Dobbs, who was taken to Saylor General Hospital shortly before she was to appear in Judge Cowen's court. Trial was set for July 23 at 10:00 A.M.

The report went on to say that Draper criticized the conduct of the police, blaming them for causing Mrs. Dobbs to become hysterical, which necessitated the trip to the hospital. Tom Miller was quoted as saying that about twenty-five or thirty workers were inside the plant, which was operating, and the story stated that eight of the city's seventeen police, almost the entire day force, were on duty at the plant.

From the outset of the strike, Phil maintained a rigid schedule to set an example for the strikers:

One simple rule that I set down for myself and organizers was that the picket lines form at 6 o'clock and that we were to be the first ones there. We would have a short meeting every morning, and every damn one of them was there, including myself. And when it rained or poured, the organizers walked the line and I walked the line, and the wetter it got, the more we were out there. And then the people could see that we weren't just a bunch of outsiders who were in there fattening ourselves at their expense. We were in there fighting — not just by word of mouth but by actual deeds. They saw that if there was anything dangerous to do, I did it or one of the other organizers did it. We never asked them to do anything that we didn't do first or that we didn't do more of. And that must have given them a feeling of confidence. They learned by example. You can't make a good picket by telling him, "You be a good picket — a good picket does so and so." You get out there and you pitch with them, that's all.

Subsequent events demonstrated that the organizers' lead had an important impact.

As the non-strikers made daily efforts to enter the plant, the strikers added a new word to their vocabularies — "scab." It was shouted and screamed at the non-strikers from the moment they appeared on the scene until they left. Scuffles became routine, even with half of the town's police force present. Several more arrests on charges of assault or disorderly conduct were made — of both organizers and rank-and-file members. Almost a hundred workers were on the picket line. When the union learned that the alley separating the loading dock at the rear of the plant from the parking lot was city and not company property, it was able to shorten the picket line and concentrate its forces at the main entrances of the mill.

Phil appealed to the officials of the Trades and Labor Council for cooperation in carrying on the strike. Through the Labor Council, union members in Saylor were urged to ask their friends or relatives who worked in the mill to participate in the picketing or, at minimum, not to cross the lines. The Labor Council leaders offered to raise funds in support of the strikers, but the offer was turned down by the union leaders on the grounds that it simply was not needed. They were asked, instead, for their moral support and, if need be, their physical support. "And I got it," Phil said. "I got it with an open hand. I got it so wonderfully that I can't imagine a better response, especially in a small community." Many members of other unions in town began showing up for picket duty either before or after going to their regular jobs. The leaders of the Trades and Labor Council were convinced that the strike of the mill workers would have an important effect upon their own union-management relationships. They were more than willing to cooperate in every way.

On the fourth day of the strike, the city attorney called a meeting in an effort to deal with picket line violence. Present were the union's attorney, the employer and his attorneys, and the city attorney. Mr. Miller and his lawyers demanded that the union agree in writing to restrain the pickets from interfering in any way with those who wanted to work in the plant. After much discussion, both sides signed a memorandum of agreement providing that the picketing strictly conform to what was permissible under the law and that all pickets desist from the following practices:

1. Going into the premises and property of the employer.
2. Blocking access from the street into the plant by means of standing pickets across the main entrance into the plant; blocking

any other entrances to the plant whether by means of the alley or any other means; blocking automobiles seeking to enter into the parking lot of the employer.
3. Using vile and abusive language and threats.
4. Assaulting the person of any employee when entering or leaving the plant.
5. Molesting any employee in any manner when entering or leaving the plant.

The document was in the form of a "gentlemen's agreement," and the organizers informed the pickets of its content and asked them to conduct themselves in accordance with it.

Yet, violence occurred again the following day as non-strikers sought to enter the plant in automobiles by way of the alley and parking lot. Several of the strikers blocked the path of at least one car and, led by sympathizing union members from other plants, tried to upset it. Police intervention prevented any injuries but resulted in new arrests. No production workers crossed the picket lines for the next three days.

When the strike was a little more than a week old, the union officials again contacted the Federal Mediation and Conciliation Service in an effort to bring about a meeting with the employer. The government agency denied the union request for intervention on the ground that

the present strained relationship between the parties concerned does not provide the proper atmosphere for our service to attempt conciliation at this time. Another week or ten days, if tempers have cooled, the Commissioner will again attempt to bring the parties together in a joint conference, conducive to reaching settlement of the existing dispute.

However, ten days later tempers were even more strained.

THE INJUNCTION

Four days after the "gentlemen's agreement" was negotiated, the company, in behalf of a group of non-striking employees, made formal application to the Circuit Court for an order restraining the union's leaders and pickets. Phil Draper, Helen Crowne, and three members of the bargaining committee were named as defendants. The company charged that the union "had wholly and completely prevented and hindered" persons from entering the plant and that persons congregating on the picket line had adopted the device of building a "solid wall of human flesh" in the approaches to the plant.

The petition asked that the pickets be restrained from maintaining a picket line in excess of twelve persons or from having a picket line of more than four persons at any one time at any of the plant entrances. Further, the petition asked that the pickets be enjoined from mass picketing, threatening employees, or "engaging in use of abusive, oppobrious or obscene language." The complaint charged that "upwards of thirty or more employees" had attempted to enter the plant on several occasions, but that they were prevented or hindered by "large numbers of pickets who ripped clothing and struck persons with picket signs." Failure to halt such activities, the company charged, would result in "substantial and irreparable injuries to the plaintiff's property and the right to earn a livelihood." The union was ordered by the Court to show cause why the injunction should not be issued. The hearing was scheduled for the following Monday.

On the same day that the company petitioned the Court, the union increased efforts to mobilize community support on its behalf. Phil offered publicly, in a half-page advertisement in the town's only newspaper, to submit the entire dispute to impartial arbitration.

WE ARE ON STRIKE AGAINST SAYLOR COMPANY

Last October we voted in a National Labor Relations Board election to have the Union represent us. We know, as does all of labor in this community, that only through a union would we be able to obtain adequate and decent wages and working conditions.

The owners of other factories in this area have learned to work with their employees through the union chosen by those employees. But the owners of the Saylor Company have not learned by the experience of others in Saylor nor do they seem to wish to learn.

They did not accept the decision of their employees in the National Labor Relations Election. They refused to deal with our union and fought that decision for five months through three delaying appeals, until required to negotiate by the National Labor Relations Board.

Nor have the last three and a half months of negotiations shown any greater desire on the part of the Saylor Company to deal fairly with us. We made certain fair demands of the Company. We asked for a general wage increase. We asked for shift differentials, paid holidays, for improvements in the vacation and insurance plans, and we asked for union security. These are the conditions which exist generally in organized industries in the United States — including our own Saylor. The Saylor Company met with us to discuss these demands, but made no effort to arrive at a fair compromise.

We waited patiently for almost nine months while the Company stalled us by means of its appeals through the National Labor Relations Board and months of fruitless negotiations. When it appeared that we would not be able to reach an agreement with the Saylor Company, we notified the Federal Mediation and Conciliation Service of the United States and requested that a Federal Conciliator be assigned. We hoped that he might be helpful in bringing both sides together and settling the dispute. That, too, failed.

When the Federal Conciliator realized that no agreement would be reached, he suggested to the Company and to the Union that they arbitrate their differences — that they jointly choose a fair-minded person and let him make a decision. *The Union agreed to arbitrate and to abide by the decisions of the arbitrator but the Saylor Company refused to arbitrate.*

Apparently the Company thought they can break up our Union by refusing to grant fair terms and by refusing to arbitrate. The Company thought that we would not want to strike nor would we be strong enough to strike. The Company was right about one thing — we did not want to strike. We did show, however, that we were strong enough to strike and determined enough to strike and carry on that strike to a successful conclusion.

Although we did not seek it, our strike is a good one and will be a successful one. Our primary interest, however, is not merely a victorious strike. It is rather a decent contract and amicable relations with the Company under the terms of such a contract. It is the thought of the Federal Conciliator and of leading citizens in this community that having failed to reach an agreement through negotiations, the parties should solve their differences amicably through arbitration. Therefore, we are still willing to arbitrate all of the issues involved.

IF THE COMPANY AGREES TO ARBITRATE, AN ARBITRATOR IS CHOSEN AND AN AGREEMENT SIGNED THAT IT WILL ACCEPT THE DECISION OF THE ARBITRATOR, WE ARE WILLING TO WITHDRAW OUR PICKET LINES, RETURN TO WORK, AND ACCEPT THE DECISION OF THE ARBITRATOR.

THE STRIKING WORKERS
At the Saylor Company

The company did not accept the union's offer to arbitrate. Indeed, the employer made no mention of the arbitration offer in a letter sent out to all employees the next day. Instead he recounted the history of the negotiations, stating the union's demands and the company's counteroffer. The letter ended by encouraging members to withdraw from the union by writing to the union's state office. It notified all workers that the plant would continue operations and that anyone wishing to work should report. However, unlike Tom Miller's previous appeal, this one produced no further defections from the union's ranks.

At the hearing on the restraining order, Phil was examined by the Court and flatly denied all allegations concerning his own participation in the violence. A number of photographs showing skirmishes between pickets and non-strikers were introduced, including one which allegedly was a picture of Phil physically restraining workers from entering the mill. The face on the picture was not clear and Phil denied that it was a picture of him.

The company's attorney questioned him at length on the number of professional organizers involved in the strike.

The Company thought we had a lot of male organizers to help us. During the injunction proceedings, I was on the witness stand, and their attorney kept lambasting me with "... whom else did you have as an organizer?" And again I enumerated our organizers over and over again, and he would ask again and again: "Are you sure that you didn't have others?" until I thought he was nuts. It was only later that I realized that the Company thought that we had prepared all sorts of goon squads and what have you. But it was just these other union guys from around town that they must have meant — these guys who would come to the line and help out. Throughout the whole strike whenever there was something to do that took a little pushing, we had plenty of local people from various other unions who volunteered.

The employer was certain that Phil had committed perjury before the Court on this point. Mr. Miller later accused the union of planning the strike while it was still meeting with the Federal Conciliator and of not bargaining in good faith. The proof, he said, was in the augmented staff of organizers in Saylor the first day of the strike.

At 6 o'clock of the morning the strike began, they had pickets out including six outside organizers, people who had not been there before. How could they have come in so soon if the strike had not been agreed upon much earlier? They must have been on the way while our meetings were going on because the only train that came into town before 6 in the morning was on its way while we were meeting. But he denied this at the hearing.

Tom Miller was amazed at Phil's conduct and greatly disappointed at the apparent willingness of his employees to follow the union's leadership.

When we had our hearings in the courtroom on the injunction, the organizer was called on to testify. He had come on our property seventy-five feet to our door and kept a girl from entering the plant. When he was asked whether he had been on our property, he denied it, and everybody in the courtroom gasped because they had seen him and they knew he was lying. When the girl he kept from entering was pointed out to him, he said he had never laid eyes on her before. We had taken pictures of him keeping her from entering, and when he was shown the pictures, he denied that he was the person. Yet, soon after, on the picket line, the people were singing that he was their leader. They were proud of him.

The employer reported that he was most impressed by the way people "can be so easily taken in by complete strangers."

Prior to the certification election, I talked to the employees four or five times, refuting things that had been told them in union bulletins. But they would believe the union organizer, not me. If I said that the wall was green and the union official said it was black, they would believe him though they could see that it was green. And these were people that I've known all my life.

Judge Murray enjoined the union and its members from committing any acts of violence on the picket line. The Court ordered that a maximum of forty-eight pickets could be at the plant at any one time, that not more than twelve pickets could be placed before any one entrance, and that the pickets must walk at least six feet apart.

While the injunction proceedings were under way, the force of city police was augmented by the County Sheriff and several of his deputies. It was the Mayor who insisted that the Sheriff assume the policing function. At first Sheriff Spencer refused on the grounds that the Mayor was specifically charged with this responsibility. When violence became a daily occurrence, the Sheriff agreed to supplement the city's police but still refused to assume principal responsibility. The Mayor was bitter about the refusal.

He runs for office and he didn't want to get the union people around here against him. He ducked his responsibility, and that made me the goat because I had to keep the city police out there. He didn't give a damn about me. His jurisdiction superseded mine because as County Sheriff he is the principal peace officer in the county. He should have come in right from the beginning when he saw there was violence out there, but he didn't. And then when he did bring in some deputies, he played politics all the way through. The deputies weren't doing their job right. They weren't neutral — they sympathized with the union people, so that got everybody in town down on the police and me.

As the strike continued, the question of which governmental agency, city or county, should pay for the policing became an important one in the town council because the cost was becoming a burden on the limited city treasury. Approximately fifteen law enforcement officers were now stationed daily at the mill — ten of them deputies assigned by the County Sheriff. The City Attorney argued that the ten should be paid $10.00 per day each, $4.00 from county funds and $6.00 from the mill owner. The city would provide two squad cars manned by three policemen. The county authorities argued that it would be difficult to justify expenditure of taxpayers' money for the protection of Miller property, but the city asserted that it was the Sheriff's duty to maintain order in the county and that the city was not excluded. The motion in the council meeting to require the mill owner to pay part of the cost of policing was defeated on the ground that this would greatly aggravate the entire situation. Finally it was decided that salaries for deputies should come from the county treasury. The issue was settled, but not without straining the relationship between the city and county law enforcement agencies.

MIRRORS, SAWS, SONGS, AND SMOKE — MORE VIOLENCE

The union's strike committee embarked on a series of projects designed to maintain morale on the picket line and further harass the thirty non-strikers who were entering the plant daily under the protection of the police and the injunction. The committee held dances and parties every weekend at the strike headquarters. At costume parties, they gave prizes for the costume judged the best caricature of the plant's managers and supervisors. Pickets began wearing these costumes, all homemade and many very colorful and imaginative, on the picket line. Dummy figures of the mill's leading supervisors were hung in effigy on lamp posts around the mill.

The pickets evolved novel methods for annoying the non-strikers inside the plant. One summer morning a striker brought a large bedroom-size mirror to the picket line and focused it so that the sun rays were reflected through the open first floor windows of the plant. Other strikers soon took up the idea. Whenever the sun shone, brilliant reflected light followed the non-striking employees at their machines.

Two of the male strikers found an old circular saw, some three feet in diameter, and mounted it on a pair of wooden horses under the windows of the main department. Using automobile axles as hammers, they pounded almost incessantly on the saw disc. The noise was deafening. One night while no strikers were around, two of the non-strikers examined the noisemaker closely.

Goose picked up that axle and banged on the God-damned thing just like those goons did. We couldn't hear for ten minutes and Goose's hand shook like a leaf. I don't understand how those people who banged on them for all those weeks didn't go deaf.

The saw-pounders and those around them didn't "go deaf" because they used earplugs. To add to the noise, others pounded on old pots and pans which they had brought to the picket line.

The combination of noisemaking, flashing light, and constant verbal abuse hurled through the open windows forced the mill management to take countermeasures. All windows were closed, but the light from the mirrors continued to be a source of annoyance. Then the management ordered all first floor windows covered with brown paper to shut out the light. The saw-pounding continued, with diminished effect, until the administrators of the City Hospital three blocks away complained that the noise was disturbing the patients.

The strikers set up a new device. Some of them got hold of large, empty fifty-gallon oil drums and a supply of old tar and tar paper. They put the drums in the alley directly in front of the loading dock and shipping room entrance, filled them with the tar and tar paper, and set the mixture afire. Every time the doors on the loading dock were opened to receive or discharge materials, the draft would draw the thick tar-laden smoke into the mill. After several days the police insisted that the fires be put out.

The pickets sang songs as they marched the line. Some were standard union songs; others were melodies taken from well-known tunes and given new lyrics by the strikers. For example, the World War I tune, "Mademoiselle from Armentières," was adapted with new lyrics, and verses were added to describe events as they occurred during the strike:

The cops are always hanging round, parlez vous
They pinch the pickets, we have found, parlez vous
In paying fines, it is Phil's joke
The union, it will never go broke
Hinkey, dinkey parlez vous.

Tom Miller is a nervous wreck, parlez vous
Tom Miller is a nervous wreck, parlez vous
Tom Miller is a nervous wreck
I bet he'd like to break our neck
Hinkey, dinkey parlez vous.

They're getting coal by parcel post, parlez vous[1]
They're getting coal by parcel post, parlez vous
Tom Miller looks just like a ghost
Paying for his parcel post
Hinkey, dinkey parlez vous.

Jim Ericson lost his lil' keys, parlez vous[2]

---

[1] The incident to which this verse refers is described on p. 91.

[2] This verse refers to an incident which occurred toward the end of the strike. Members of the Teamsters Union refused to cross the union picket line, and the mill's only pickup truck could not carry all of the materials moving in and out of the plant. One mid-morning, the company's purchasing agent attempted to drive his car out of the plant area. He was stopped by a wall of strikers who demanded that he open the trunk of his car for inspection. While he was arguing with the pickets, one of the strikers removed the keys from the ignition. No one would admit to the police on duty that he had the keys. Meanwhile the argument about opening the trunk continued. The keys were produced when the supervisor finally agreed to let the strikers inspect the contents of the trunk. The trunk was found to contain several large boxes of finished products. The pickets refused to permit the supervisor to leave the plant until the "contraband" was removed. The police were reluctant to insist that the supervisor be allowed to take the finished products out since that action almost certainly would have provoked considerable violence. When the bundles were removed, the purchasing agent was allowed to drive his car away.

Jim Ericson lost his lil' keys, parlez vous
Jim Ericson lost his lil' keys
He got them back when he said "PLEASE"
Hinkey, dinkey parlez vous.

They took those bundles out of the car, parlez vous
They took those bundles out of the car, parlez vous
They took those bundles out of the car
You bet they didn't travel far
Hinkey, dinkey parlez vous.

The scabs are having a heck of a time, parlez vous
The scabs are having a heck of a time, parlez vous
The scabs are having a heck of a time
Trying to break our picket line
Hinkey, dinkey parlez vous.

Other verses dealt with various supervisors, efforts by the company to continue production, and the signing of a contract.

Another song was sung to the melody of "Give Me a Little Kiss, Will Ya, Huh?":

Give us a decent raise, will ya, huh?
Just a decent raise, will ya, huh?
Gosh oh gee, why do you refuse?
We can't see what you got to lose.
Oh, give us a decent raise, will ya, huh?
Why do you wanna make us blue?
We wouldn't say a word if we were asking for the world,
But what's a little raise between Tom and the girls?
Oh, give us a little raise, will ya, huh?
So we can buy a Buick, too.

As the strike continued into August and September, there were days when rain and even light snow fell. On one such day, quite late in the strike, the pickets put these words to the tune of "Rudolph the Red-Nosed Reindeer":

We are the red nose pickets,
Walking in the rain and snow,
We are the red nose pickets,
Can't you see our noses glow?

We are the red nose pickets,
Cheerful as the morning sun,

When the scabbies hear us holler,
Golly how we make them run!

When the scabs crawl into work
They holler for the cops.
Miller, cops and deputies
Will never make us stop.

We are the red nose pickets,
Walking on the picket line.
We will never, never give up
'Til we get our contract signed!

After the picketing injunction was issued, a new song was heard on the line. The words were set to a melody that had been popular a few years before, "Pistol-Packing Mama — Lay That Pistol Down":

Oh, lay that injunction down, Tom,
Lay that injunction down,
Pick up the union contract
And lay that injunction down.

 Violence continued. Several non-strikers reported to police that "unknown persons" had broken windows in their homes, thrown carpet tacks on their driveways, and splashed white paint on their automobiles. The pickets had devised a way of filling egg shells with different colors of paint. They used pins to drill small holes in the shells, drained out the yolk and white, and used a medical syringe to refill the shells with paint. They threw the eggs at non-strikers' cars and at the doors and windows of their homes.

 A picket charged a non-striker with reckless driving, charging that he deliberately tried to run her down as he drove into the mill. Four pickets were arrested on charges of making unnecessary noise — sounding automobile horns unnecessarily and using the circular saw as a noisemaker. An organizer was arrested for allegedly using abusive language. One of the organizers assigned to the strike by the Chicago office of the international union was in Saylor police court twice in as many days, once for using abusive language and the second time on an assault and battery charge. Two weeks later she was arrested again and charged with property destruction — breaking the rear window of a car driven by a non-striker. A few days later seven men, leading a crowd estimated to number at least 150, attempted to upset a car driven by a male non-striker and occupied by several women workers.

The non-strikers were rescued by police. The Sheriff reported that he did not recognize any of the men who were lifting the car. The following week the police took five men and one woman into custody for attempting to prevent the unloading of a mill shipment at the Railway Express Company warehouse. They were warned that if such incidents occurred again, the persons involved would be arrested. "They've got to do as I tell them," the Sheriff stated. An organizer was arrested on a charge of inciting to riot and unlawful assembly when "in a violent and tumultuous manner he threw stones at the automobile of a supervisor at the mill."

The arrests seemed to take on a fixed pattern. Many of the warrants were issued late on Friday afternoons rather than earlier in the day or on other days. Phil concluded that it was a deliberate police tactic designed to jail union members over a weekend when no court was sitting and when it was difficult to secure bond.

One incident, typical of others, illustrates Phil's problem. About 4:30 on a Friday afternoon, he was in Chuck's hotel room preparing to leave for a strike rally when two policemen rapped on the door and announced that they had a warrant for Chuck's arrest on a charge of picket line violence. During the conversation Phil learned that the police also had a warrant for the arrest of a woman striker and were about to look for her. Phil phoned the local bonding company to arrange bail for Chuck, but since it was after 5 o'clock, he was unable to reach a bondsman. As Phil, Chuck, and the two officers were leaving the hotel on their way to jail, Phil noticed another woman striker in the hotel lobby. He quickly and privately told her to go to Cora's house immediately to warn her and to get her out of town — across the state line to a neighboring city where it would require formal extradition proceedings to arrest her.

Phil was particularly concerned about keeping the strikers out of jail, and he did not want to give the police the satisfaction of having their "Friday afternoon arrest" plan work out successfully. He was not as concerned about the professional organizers since going to jail was part of their jobs. Yet in this instance he was determined to spare Chuck a weekend in jail if he could. He called several local judges and justices of the peace, but was unable to find one who would set bail and sign the necessary release papers. He was not surprised since he had concluded that the issues in the strike situation were too hot and that there was too much political pressure in support of the Millers. Phil eventually located a justice of the peace who was at odds with the city administration and who agreed to set bail and execute the necessary documents. The city attorney, who had been notified, objected on the grounds that a justice of the peace had no authority in the case, but the justice insisted that he did have authority and released Chuck. Phil brought Cora back to Saylor the following Monday and she appeared voluntarily before the sitting judge. Thus Phil managed to keep both of them out of jail.

One Saturday evening, the pickets discovered that a non-striking worker was acting as a plant guard. They suspected that he was preparing to receive an important shipment of raw materials and quickly passed the word around town. In a very short time more than 150 persons gathered by the mill entrance. Meanwhile the non-striker locked himself inside the plant. The crowd shouted, "We want Gizlo, we want Gizlo . . . ," as they threw stones at the building. Several windows and light fixtures were broken. The police on duty called the Sheriff for additional forces and, after inspecting the situation, Sheriff Spencer summoned company officials to an emergency conference at the police station. He told them bluntly that "they faced a wrecked plant by Sunday morning if Gizlo is not removed." The management agreed to replace Gizlo with a policeman, and the police escorted the non-striker to his home some seven miles out in the country.

After Phil appealed to the crowd to disperse peacefully, most of the people left, but a few pickets remained at the scene all night. The Sheriff reported later that many outsiders as well as striking workers were in the crowd. Several evenings later three of the strike leaders drove out to Gizlo's farm home to attempt to convince him to stay away from the plant during the strike. They parked their car on a dirt road near the house and approached on foot. When they were greeted by two shotgun blasts, they beat a hasty retreat. No one was hit, but the incident clearly indicated to the strikers that the breach between themselves and at least one of their former co-workers was wide indeed. They did not make another attempt to talk to Gizlo.

Picket line violence occurred sporadically for about four months. Strikers and organizers were arrested for a variety of offenses ranging from malicious mischief to inciting to riot. Crowds of local citizens often gathered across the street from the mill entrances to watch for any excitement. Many were relatives and friends of those directly involved; others were simply curious sightseers; still others were trade unionists from other plants who voluntarily offered aid to the mill strikers. Never once, however, was the leading actor in the entire strike arrested. Phil's numerous provocative acts went unheeded by the police.

THE UNITED LABOR COMMITTEE

After the injunction was issued, Phil increased his efforts to mobilize the support of the townspeople on behalf of the union. He had been in almost daily contact with officials of the Trades and Labor Council and kept them fully informed of the union's activity. He addressed numerous meetings of various local unions in Saylor and neighboring towns. During these meetings and discussions he constantly urged the trade unionists to use whatever influence they had with mill workers to support the union's cause. He did not directly attack the Miller family or their power in the community. When he referred to the employer or his family, it was in general terms — the company. Yet he constantly sought to point out that the strike and all later events need not have happened if "the company" had wanted it otherwise.

He suggested to the leadership of the Labor Council and to officials of the several local unions affiliated with the CIO that a United Labor Committee might be useful. The suggestion quickly bore fruit, and a committee composed of representatives of twenty-three local unions in Saylor and two neighboring towns was organized. Its sole purpose at the time was to aid the strikers, and union leaders were invited to speak both on the picket line and during meal hours in strike headquarters.

More than a thousand people gathered in the City Park to hear Phil speak at a mass meeting arranged by the committee. He reviewed the many delays which preceded the contract negotiations and charged the company with responsibility for the delays and with lack of good faith in its negotiations. He claimed that the strike was forced upon the union by the company's refusal to compromise and its failure to agree to fair terms which would have made a contract possible. He further emphasized the company's refusal to arbitrate. He insisted that the court injunction in no way had affected the conduct of the strike. If anything, he said, the strikers now were more determined than ever to continue their fight to a successful conclusion.

Several members of the United Labor Committee also spoke and the invocation was given by a leading Catholic priest of the area. The meeting was a huge success from the union's point of view; nothing like it had ever happened before in Saylor. Indeed, this was the first time both AFL- and CIO-affiliated unions had ever engaged in a joint enterprise.

The various unions in Saylor cooperated with the mill strikers in even more important ways. The Teamsters Union respected the strikers' picket lines, and all deliveries to the mill were cut off. This left only the mill's small pickup truck to bring in or ship out mill materials, and the non-union truck driver was followed and harassed whenever he left the mill. Shipments of materials to the struck plant began coming in by Railway Express.

After the strike had been going on for about three months, Phil learned that business had fallen off about 20 per cent at the Miller Brothers Department Store, the largest retail merchandising establishment in an area of about 2,500 square miles. The union found that at least some of the townspeople were boycotting the store, although neither the United Labor Committee nor the strikers had made an attempt to initiate or urge it. Both groups encouraged the boycott, however, once it was under way.

Leaders of the committee, under Phil's prodding and direction, sought ways to increase the pressure on the employer through the department store. However, they needed to be extremely cautious since the store had no direct or legal connection with the mill. Sustained activity directed against the store in an effort to increase pressure upon the mill's management would have been a clear-cut violation of the secondary boycott bans in the Taft-Hartley Act.

Phil used an indirect method; he told the regional officials of the AFL Retail Clerks' Union about the unorganized department store which employed several hundred persons in Saylor. The Retail Clerks agreed to attempt an organization drive and sent a representative to

Saylor to seek union recognition from the store's management. Of course the employer refused. The Clerks' Union posted pickets in front of the store entrances and delivery docks, proclaiming that the Miller Brothers Department Store did not employ union labor. The Teamsters Union respected the picket line, and the store was forced to hire additional non-union drivers to get merchandise into and out of the store. It was reported that business at the store fell off by almost 60 per cent.

Friday evening is the traditional shopping time for residents of the Saylor area. The town takes on a holiday atmosphere as crowds converge in its main shopping district and the Miller Brothers' store. The farm people of the area come to town on Friday evenings to shop and perhaps to attend a movie. On two Friday evenings, the United Labor Committee, again prodded by Phil, organized demonstrations in support of the AFL Retail Clerks' Union. Approximately a thousand pickets formed a continuous line around the entire city block occupied by the store. They carried signs urging shoppers not to buy at the store. Phil specifically instructed the mill strikers to stay out of the demonstration so that if the secondary boycott question should be raised subsequently, the union would be able to point out that it had no connection whatever with the demonstrations. Business at the store practically came to a standstill each Friday evening. Other merchants in the downtown area complained that business in general declined sharply while the demonstrators were parading and the citizenry gathered to watch the spectacle. The town's newspaper estimated that several thousand shoppers gathered in the square to watch. Automobile traffic through the downtown area was completely tangled.

The annual Trades and Labor Council picnic was held on Labor Day in the City Park. The city band, a group of acrobats, students from a local dancing school, and several amateur boxers provided entertainment. Soft drinks, hot dogs, and the usual picnic fare were served. The crowd was estimated to number well over a thousand. Phil was the chief speaker. He again outlined the issues in the strike and said that an amicable outcome was as important to the community as it was to the strikers since wages and working conditions in the mill inevitably affected wages and conditions in all other local firms. Although Labor Day celebrations had been held before in Saylor, this was the largest and most successful. It indicated to the strikers that a large section of the community supported their cause. The enthusiasm developed at the picnic carried over to the following meeting of the Trades and Labor Council when a resolution was passed calling for a city-wide half-day holiday of all union labor in support of the strikers. The pressure was mounting.

THE TURNING POINT

It was now late September. The cold weather of fall and winter was approaching and the coal supply at the mill was running short. One Saturday afternoon, while pickets were absent from the scene, a truckload of coal was delivered by a firm which employed non-union drivers. All truck markings were covered. The coal was dumped behind the mill, and the driver, in a hurry to leave before being discovered, made no arrangements to deposit his cargo in the basement of the factory.

A passing striker soon discovered the delivery and called Phil, who arrived at the mill in time to see the truck drive off after dumping a second load. He and the striker followed the truck to a neighboring city where the driver headed for a police station after discovering that he was being followed. Phil went into the station behind the driver and asked him for the name of the coal company which employed him. When the driver refused to answer, Phil went outside to the truck and ripped off the paper covering the firm's name. His next step was to notify the Teamsters' local leaders. As a result, union drivers employed by other dealers agreed to refuse to deliver coal to the Miller Brothers Department Store, and Teamster officials urged their members to stop dealing with the non-union company. Four loads of coal had been ordered by the mill, but only two were delivered. From this time until the end of the strike, the mill was picketed around the clock every day.

Non-strikers rigged a number of large tarpaulins around the coal pile behind the mill. The following night someone threw two large bags of dry cement over the coal, making it useless until several days later when it was thoroughly washed several times and carted inside the mill by wheelbarrow. The tarpaulin curtain shielded the non-strikers from the glares and jibes of the pickets.

Since the company could no longer buy coal in Saylor, it looked for supplies from outlying communities. A supervisor arranged with a Saylor resident, who had no connection with the strike, to buy coal from a dealer some thirty miles away. One truckload was delivered and dumped in the intermediary's back yard. From this point, the mill's supervisors and some of the non-strikers packaged the coal in thirty-pound boxes, carried it by car to the Saylor Post Office, and mailed it to the mill. The company believed that this method of delivery could not be stopped since the coal was mail in custody of an agency of the federal government. Some of the pickets suspected that coal had somehow been delivered to the mill since there was evidence of dust on the receiving dock. Phil laughed at their suspicions, saying that nobody could get coal delivered by mail. But a picket captain insisted that coal must be coming in by mail since all other avenues had been blocked. A friend who worked in the Post Office confirmed his suspicions.

Phil immediately protested to the local postmaster, charging that the Post Office was directly aiding one side in a labor dispute. The local postmaster checked with the Chicago postmaster and was told that under Post Office regulations, unusual items of mail not ordinarily delivered to a firm could not be handled during a strike. The coal deliveries were stopped.

In the meantime the company continued to purchase coal from the same out-of-town firm and box it in the same way. While negotiations were proceeding with the Post Office, several tons of packaged coal were delivered to the freight platform of the Northwestern Railroad in Saylor. Miller Brothers Department Store trucks, escorted by some Sheriff's deputies, picked up the packages and deposited them in the mill's coal chute. Phil discovered what was happening only when a railroad employee, who was a member of the Railway Clerks Union, phoned him the details.

When Phil arrived at the railroad freight office, he found several score packages of coal on the freight platform. He told the freight-master that the railroad was permitting the mill to use it to break a strike because the coal was not regular freight consigned to the railroad. He asked the freight-master to reject it. When the freight-master refused, Phil called the railroad's Chicago district office and insisted that orders be given to the Saylor agent to stop accepting the coal parcels. If the railroad would not do this, he said, the union would consider it a direct party to the mill dispute and would picket the Saylor freight and passenger stations.

An exchange of telephone calls between Phil, the Saylor freight office, and the district office went on through the day. In the meantime the department store trucks continued to pick up the packages at the freight platform. Phil recruited two carloads of pickets who took up positions nearby. He and two other organizers stopped a truck from backing into the freight platform by standing in its path. The driver left without coal when he realized that he would run down the organizers if he attempted to back his truck in to the platform. There were no police present at the time, but shortly afterward a contingent from the Sheriff's force arrived and parked some distance away. However, the police refused to interfere with the pickets blocking the pickup trucks.

Higher officials of the railroad came to Saylor later that day. After several hours of discussion with Phil, who continually threatened to picket the station, the officials agreed to put the coal aside and declare it impounded. It was not to be released until the strike was over or until the union okayed the movement. Indeed, it was not released until the strike ended with a signed contract. Then it was brought directly into the plant so that steam pressure could be brought up and the plant reopened.

The coal impasse was one of the major turning points in the strike. With winter rapidly approaching, the mill could not be operated without coal, and the strikers knew it. They also knew that the company was heating workplaces with portable electric heaters and that nonstrikers had to wear sweaters and coats as they worked. They felt that there might be some hope of bringing the employer to terms if the coal supply were not replenished.

Devising strategies to block the coal became a welcome diversion for the strikers and a source of renewed morale in a strike which had dragged on for more than three months with no apparent progress. The direct issues in the conflict became submerged, and coal became a new symbol for the entire struggle. The critical situation with regard to coal at the mill and the mounting pressure on the Miller store combined to compel the employer to renew negotiations with the union.

NEGOTIATIONS RESUMED

Phil's position from the very beginning was that constant efforts had to be made to negotiate with the employer. He considered this fundamental strategy. "The people had to believe and had to know that the union was trying to settle the strike." Phil continually pressed for negotiations through the Federal Mediation and Conciliation Service. On two occasions formal meetings were held in another city, and on several other occasions mediators talked to Phil and Tom Miller separately in Saylor. "We kept after the Federal Mediator to keep his finger in the pie so the people would see that we were trying to settle it."

During the seventh week of the strike a meeting was arranged at which Mr. Miller and his attorneys sat down with an international vice-president, Phil, and the local strike committee. A company attorney spoke on the subject of strike violence for about ten minutes. When he finished, the vice-president spoke, saying, in effect, that the Miller family was very rich and powerful in Saylor but that the union could buy and sell all the Millers in the state. For every dollar the Millers had to spend, he continued, the union had at least ten, and if the company wanted to continue the strike on this basis, the union was more than prepared. And as for the picket line violence, he added, "What else could you expect in a war which is what a strike is? What do you expect the pickets to do — walk on the line with flowers for the scabs?" The local strike committee was much impressed and found renewed hope for the success of the strike and renewed faith in the union leadership.

But no progress was made toward settling the conflict. Another effort to resume negotiations was made a few weeks later when emissaries of the employer approached the Sheriff to arrange a meeting between the company and the union. Phil notified the Sheriff that he would be happy to meet with the company any time and any place. But the company now stated a condition for the meeting: they were ready to meet with the strikers provided that Phil was not present.

Phil raised the question with the strike committee: "you can do what you want, but you see what they're trying to do. They're trying to break you and me apart." He left the committee to discuss the matter. The committee members unanimously agreed that they would meet with the employer only if Phil was present and the Sheriff was so notified. This condition was unacceptable to the employer and the brief contact was broken off for the time being.

Meanwhile Phil thought it was wise to bolster the morale of the strikers again, particularly since he was sure that the employer would continue efforts to split the strikers from their leadership and negotiate a "private" settlement. Accordingly, he invited one of the union vice-presidents and the Midwest general organizer to Saylor to address the strikers at a meeting in strike headquarters. The general organizer, a very effective speaker, told the audience that all of the resources of their union of over 400,000 workers were at the disposal of the 125 mill strikers. The union vice-president added that the international would never withdraw from the Saylor conflict and was prepared to finance the strike until the union's demands were won. They sought to leave the impression that a relatively small operator such as the mill owner had little chance against the combined resources of the powerful union. Only grit and determination were needed on the part of people directly involved.

The employer's effort to split the union ranks from its leadership failed completely. However, the attempt indicated to the union's leadership that the company was being pressed to the wall and was seeking ways to end the strike. Other developments confirmed this feeling.

The firm's Chicago and New York sales offices were picketed by union people, and the company's salesmen were becoming increasingly dissatisfied. Phil reported it this way:

In a strike, especially when it runs as long as this one did, you're always letting out feelers. You don't let out the feelers in your own name, but you get some guy, maybe a lawyer or another manufacturer who knows somebody who knows somebody else to say, "Why can't we do something? I think I know these union guys and maybe we can do something." The company was doing this too through their salesmen and people who their salesmen knew in the industry in Chicago and New York. Those of us who were directly involved in the strike weren't directly involved in these feelers — we kept ourselves out at this stage. This is a very diplomatic sort of procedure, something like international relations with neutrals during a war. But through this kind of thing both sides maintained some kind of contact with each other. All the feelers we let out in the beginning were chopped off, and we stopped sending them out for a while. But when the coal situation got so rough and the community support became so evident, it seemed to us that the company realized they were either going to have to settle it or go out of business. We heard from Chicago and New York that their salesmen were getting fed up — getting ready to quit because no products were getting through. We were hoping that this would occur.

As a result of these "feelers," a meeting was arranged in Chicago between Chicago officials of the union and the mill's attorneys. No immediate progress was made, but negotiations were not broken off entirely this time.

In mid-October, when the strike was entering its fourth month, a new development occurred. The Mayor appointed a Citizens Committee to meet with representatives of both sides to try to end the struggle. Phil initiated the move by dropping hints to the Trades and Labor Council officials, to clergymen with whom he had good contact, and to others. He did not anticipate that a citizens group could really be instrumental in settling the strike, but it was part of his strategy to keep the situation in constant motion.

The president of the Saylor Chamber of Commerce also thought that the committee idea was good, but his feelings were mixed.

Draper has got the people all stirred up. I don't know what it is — if it is the people who worked at the mill for twenty-five years suddenly got up and found that their wages are very low, conditions bad, or that Draper has a spell over them or what. You know how emotional women can get, and that place has mostly women working there. Draper is an outsider who came here just to stir things up. He doesn't have any stake in this community, and what the hell does he care what he does to this town. He doesn't care a thing about Saylor. That's his profession and he knows all the tricks in the trade about how to stir people up. He came in here driving a big Cadillac and started to tear the place apart.[3] If it lasted much longer, there would have been a committee of fifteen men in town that would have run him out and told him to stay out.

But still, he felt, the situation had gotten out of hand and it should not have been permitted to continue. Though his private sympathies were with Tom Miller, he recognized that every effort had to be made

---

[3] At the time of these events Phil drove a two-year-old Dodge.

to end the strike. Yet he was reluctant to involve the Chamber as an organization.

The Chamber of Commerce can't mix in politics, and this had become a political issue because of the relationship of the Millers and the store to the Chamber and the community as a whole. It would have created dissension amongst ourselves.

He called the manager of the store, one of Tom Miller's brothers, to ask if there was anything he could do as a private individual.

He asked me what I had in mind. I told him that it was my idea to get a group of reputable businessmen in the town, unbiased people, who spoke for the community as a whole and see what we could do. We didn't know what we could do, but I wanted to experiment and find out. He asked me who I had in mind for such a committee, and I named a few and he named a few. We wanted to show both sides that the community had a stake in this and that it wasn't their private war. We wanted to talk to one side and then the other separately and see what we could do to get them together.

The Mayor agreed to sponsor the effort. He appointed five of the town's leading citizens, all businessmen but one, to attempt mediation. The pastor of the Methodist church was selected as chairman. The Mayor issued the following statement to the press:

The strike at the Saylor Company is now going into its 13th week and should give the people of this community more than passing concern. It affects not only the economy of a city of our size, but has disrupted the harmony which should prevail between some of our citizens. I have waited hopefully for several weeks for an adjustment of the dispute between the parties through a compromise settlement. This failed to materialize and it is quite evident that negotiations between the parties are now at a standstill and such a condition will exist unless some attempt is made by an intervening third party. It must be an effort to bring the parties involved together in an attempt to effectuate an amicable settlement. With this in mind, I have appointed a Citizens' Committee to meet with representatives of both employees and employer immediately and assist them in negotiations toward bringing about an early settlement of their differences. The members of the committee have agreed to serve at my request as a public service to Saylor. I have confidence that my selection will meet with the approval of the parties as they are leaders in various professions and businesses, and have no direct or indirect interest in the matters in the dispute.

The chairman of the committee told Phil about the new development and asked his cooperation. Phil replied that the union would be very happy to have such a group intervene.

The pastor forced me into the position where I had to open up with him. I figured that I'm better off talking to a minister than I was to a businessman — that I could trust him more. And I told him that I was speaking to him off the record, but the situation was such that there was the possibility of a settlement and, off the record, I would appreciate it if the entire committee would stand back until they were needed, if they were needed. And he understood, and promised to keep out of it until we had a chance to settle it ourselves.

The committee never met. As a result of a rapidly moving series of events in Chicago the following day, the company moved to negotiate directly with the strikers and their representatives.

The manager of the company's Chicago sales office and the union's Midwest general organizer met on a Chicago streetcar. The sales manager told the union official that the company wanted to settle and that it had retained a new attorney with considerable experience in the industry and close ties with one of the unions in the industry. The new attorney also knew the union's lawyer, who had been involved from the beginning in the Saylor strike.

A meeting was arranged for October 24th in Chicago with top union officials, Phil, and their attorney representing the union, and Tom Miller and his new attorney representing the company. They reached agreement quickly, and after the local union strike committee was flown from Saylor to Chicago to sit in on the discussion, the parties arrived at a general settlement on all issues except the union shop. The company wanted two years from the time the contract was signed before the union shop was to become effective; the union insisted on six months. After the question was discussed for some time, the union vice-president met privately with Tom Miller. Ten minutes later they emerged arm-in-arm from the former's office. At Mr. Miller's request, the vice-president had given his word that the demonstrations at the Miller Department Store would be stopped immediately if the company conceded on the union shop question. The parties finally agreed on a compromise — installation of the union shop in ten months.

Under the terms of the agreement, the company recognized the functions of the shop chairman and the piecework price adjustment committee. The new grievance procedure included an arbitration step, and a plant-wide seniority system was installed. Provisions were made to adjust the pay of workers who were shifted from one job to another so that they would not lose any income. A minimum of four hours' call-in pay was stipulated. The company agreed to develop an equitable piece-rate system by consulting with an engineer from the union's staff as well as one chosen by management. Piece rates in all departments would be increased while the piecework system was being studied. Adjustments were made in vacation benefits, and a 10 per cent across-the-board wage increase for all workers was granted.

Phil called Helen in Saylor to ask her to announce and publicize a settlement ratification meeting for the following evening. Phil and the local union bargaining committee took the first available transportation to Saylor and came before about 125 union members to describe the terms of the agreement. After a very short discussion, a motion was made to accept the contract as proposed. The vote was enthusiastically affirmative. The union and the strikers viewed the settlement as a clean victory. After almost a year and a half of continuous effort, including a bitter fourteen-week strike, the union had a contract.

6

Tactics of Organizing

Formation of a local union which can win collective bargaining rights and establish itself as a relatively permanent organization in its plant or industry depends upon a combination of circumstances. Typically, union organization occurs where there is widespread dissatisfaction among the workers, leadership devoted to the idea of unionism, and favorable economic and political conditions. The success of the effort is enhanced if there is available in the critical early period the guidance of an experienced and resourceful union representative who has behind him the prestige and financial resources of a powerful organization. Generally it is the organizer who seeks out promising situations in his assigned territory, stimulates the organization of local unions, and continues to furnish assistance as the new groups require it.

In some instances, formal leadership by a professional organizer is crucial. In others, leadership may emerge almost spontaneously from an informal group of disaffected workers. In some situations, the most able, experienced, and articulate professional organizer may be totally unsuccessful. In others, no formal leadership at all may be required.

There are instances where unions have been organized by professionals and have achieved employer recognition without one of the affected workers knowing about it. A so-called "back door agreement" has been written many times between a union business agent and an employer who chooses to do business with him rather than with a representative of another union.

Unions also have been organized by non-professionals working on a full-time job in a plant. Their organizing activity may consist of nothing more than the constant pressure of fellow workers in the shop, in the cafeteria, during rest periods, or over a glass of beer after working hours. Such activity may go on for a considerable period of time before it bears fruit. Or it may never result in unionization.

During the middle and late 1930's, tens of thousands of workers flocked into unions, often without the aid or leadership of professional organizers. The New Deal and desperation born of the depression provided an atmosphere in which unionism, protected by the Wagner Act, could flourish. Without doubt, the Roosevelt administration's proclaimed sympathy to unionism and the deflation of big business omniscience contributed to the spectacular growth of unions during this era. Throughout many parts of the country, particularly in the automobile, steel, and electrical manufacturing industries, workers formed unions faster than professional organizers could officially enroll them.

In contrast, the CIO's 1946-47 southern organizing drive, "Operation Dixie," was a costly failure. Hundreds of professional organizers spent millions of dollars without increasing union membership by any significant number. Techniques which were effective during the 1930's proved inapplicable in this vastly different situation. An organizer working in Fayetteville, Tennessee, Elba, Alabama, or Alexandria City, Georgia, soon found that he was in an environment politically hostile to unionism despite the legal protection of the Wagner Act.[1] In comparable situations, the most resourceful organizer, backed by the most powerful national union, would have no success whatsoever.

By the time the Taft-Hartley Act was passed in 1947, the general climate of opinion in the country had changed considerably. The period of social reform had come to an end and economic prosperity had returned. Many provisions of the Act were being used by employers to stop organization cold. Union organizing became very difficult not only in the new industrial South but also in many places in the

---

[1] For a discussion of the violent opposition to the 1946-47 organizing drive, see Harry A. Millis and Emily Clark Brown, *From the Wagner Act to Taft-Hartley* (Chicago, 1950), particularly pp. 639-54.

old industrial North and Middle West. With the end of the upswing of the 1930's and the beginning of a new period heralded by the passage of the Taft-Hartley Act, the professional union organizer became an increasingly important arm of the union which hired him. No longer were workers flocking into unions in spontaneous groups. Unionizing now required the talents of the professional who was able to sell an idea.

Typically, a condition of individual unrest among workers, a feeling of dissatisfaction with existing factory conditions, is the prelude to successful organization of a union. Such a condition usually does not emerge spontaneously. Rather it is the result of an accumulation of complaints and grievances against management and its agents. The process may continue for a relatively long period of time before a move toward unionization emerges.

The absence of suitable channels which might function to relieve the anxiety or frustration-producing situation leads the individual workers to become susceptible to appeals that will offer the most satisfaction. New conceptions of what is "right" develop to produce new hopes and wishes. Rejection of at least certain aspects of the social system of the factory represents the potential motivating condition which may lead the individual to join a union.

But a condition of individual unrest is insufficient. It must become social; that is, it must be communicated. It becomes a social condition when other individuals detect the manifestations of dissatisfaction and respond to them sympathetically.[2] Organization may occur when the aroused tension is focused and comes to be defined as requiring behavior along certain lines.

Within this general explanation of why workers join unions, specific reasons may be found in the concrete, everyday conditions of a worker's life and work experience. His hopes and fears in his role as a worker center about such matters as employment, wages and hours, methods of payment, and the like. He is vitally concerned with those matters which touch his present and future well-being and the economic, social, and ethical standards and conditions which determine these matters.[3]

---

[2] See Robert E. Park and E. W. Burgess, *Introduction to the Science of Sociology* (Chicago, 1942), p. 866.

[3] See Robert Franklin Hoxie, *Trade Unionism in the United States* (New York, 1917).

The worker develops a social viewpoint as he attempts to comprehend and solve his problems; that is, he comes to interpret the social situation as he views it from the standpoint of his particular experiences and needs. Out of this comes a set of beliefs concerning what should and could be done to better his situation. Yet, the worker's interpretation does not provide for group action until it becomes shared with others. A common interpretation of the dissatisfactions and the social reality from which they stem may come about gradually, or it may be the apparent outcome of some immediate crisis in the lives of the workers concerned. More often, though, a common sentiment crystallizes as a leader from among the disaffected workers or an outside professional labor organizer is able to articulate the discontent and offer a positive solution in the name of "unionism."

But whether the workers' new conceptions arise from a crisis situation or develop gradually with the guidance of a professional organizer, the result may be the same. A social group may be constituted, marked off by a more or less unified viewpoint regarding the situation which brought it into being. As soon as this has occurred, group action becomes possible.[4]

The mill workers were dissatisfied with specific issues in their work situation. Most of them felt that the general level of earnings was too low; many were aware that wages were higher in organized factories in the area. Some workers complained about the dilution of the incentive payment after increases were applied to the guaranteed minimum rate. Some were dissatisfied with the entire piecework system. Some charged the supervisors with favoritism in assigning tasks and setting rates under the prevailing method of work distribution. Many

---

[4] George Herbert Mead has offered a similar interpretation: "The process through which a union is organized is fundamentally a process of the coming to a new self-consciousness on the part of the laborer in the changing industrial conditions in which he finds himself. . . . The individual laborer can become conscious of himself only in so far as he realizes himself in the common attitudes of the group over against the employing class or another group of workers, and the whole history of the development of society has shown that this negative attitude must precede any consciousness of common interests which bind the group to others in society. The trade union is then one step in the process of socializing the laborers brought under the modern process of industry, and goes through the same stages through which the community itself has passed in advancing from hostile groups into a conscious organization of diverse but interacting elements of society." Quoted in Hoxie, p. 57.

felt that it was hopeless to complain about unfair rates or unequal distribution of work because they were convinced that they would either be fired or ignored if they did.

The majority of the workers who played leading roles in the organizing effort possessed some degree of conviction regarding the legitimacy and utility of a union as an agency which would advance and protect their interests in the mill.[5] Most of them either had had previous personal experience as members of unions in other work situations or had relatives who were union members. Possessing some general concept of the role of a union in a workplace, they were able to view their own disaffections in the light of what "ought to be" and the union as an agency for achieving these expectations. Unionization became an acceptable solution to individual problems when the individual worker became conscious of his discontent in relation to other workers whom he knew as union members.

In this process, the union organizers played a crucial role. They did not create the unrest, the dissatisfaction and frustration. They probed for symptoms, brought them to the surface, emphasized them, and sought to place the responsibility for them with the employer. They sought details of each worker's life experience in the factory and used these experiences to point out injustices suffered at work. Their task was to convince the worker that his sense of grievance was justified and could be removed by unionization. When the organizers found substantial individual dissatisfaction, they tried to transform it into a group condition and to channel it in the direction of group action through formation of a union. They built up further grievances by defining and redefining existing dissatisfactions. They emphasized the justice of the workers' claims by bringing out comparisons with conditions in unionized plants. They tried to convince the workers that they,

---

[5] Similar findings were made by the author in another study. "In any unorganized plant, the presence in numbers of workers with pro-union sympathies, whether because of family background, prior union membership, or unpleasant experiences at the plant, will materially affect the success or failure of any organizing drive. Workers such as these are among the first to join a union and usually become its nucleus. On the other hand, workers without any previous pro-union background are among the most difficult to organize and often join only after the union achieves status and power." See Joel Seidman, Jack London, and Bernard Karsh, "Why Workers Join Unions," *Annals of the American Academy of Political and Social Science*, CCLXXIV (March, 1950), 75-85.

too, could be spared their unhappy experiences if they formed a union. Their purposes were to bring the workers whom they were attempting to proselytize to the point where they would reject the existing situation as a "normal way of life" and to transform the unorganized amalgam of disaffected individuals into a group bound together around the idea of "union." Grievances then would cease to be an individual matter and would become a collective concern. In this task, however, the organizers served as much more than a catalytic agent. They brought with them their experiences as organizers and the economic and political resources of a national organization. Further, they were the principal architects of the objectives and tactics of the local group until it gained enough experience to share in directing its affairs.

The union, particularly in areas away from the metropolitan centers of union organization, may be only an abstraction of which an organizer is the only tangible embodiment. Although the workers may be told that he represents a body of perhaps hundreds of thousands of members, they are apt to respond, particularly during the crucial early period of the campaign, according to their estimate of the organizer himself. Ideally, the union organizer does nothing that will engender hostility toward himself in the community or among the workers whom he is trying to organize. Whatever his personal views on politics, religion, sex, and temperance, he will not air them if they run counter to prevailing sentiments in the community or in the specific group of employees. The personality of the organizer is important, for he sells himself along with, and perhaps as much as, his union. He must inspire confidence, and he must be the kind of a person whom the workers would admire and like to have as a friend. His task is greatly facilitated if he is enough like the employees in socioeconomic background, national origin, and similar respects to be accepted readily by them as a friend and associate.

In all of these respects, Helen was admirably suited for work among the Saylor Company employees. Her home was in an iron-mining and lumber community north of Saylor. Her father and husband had been miners and active in union organizing efforts in their community. She had worked for fifteen years in the same industry as the Saylor company employees, filling a variety of unpaid local union offices, including president, before joining the organizing staff of the union. A middle-aged, stout, gray-haired, and motherly person, she readily inspired confidence among the mill women. Essentially, she had the same small town frame of reference as the Saylor workers and understood them and their problems. She spoke in the same colloquial tones characteristic of the Upper Midwest area and could be identified easily as a native of the region. In substance, she "spoke the language of the people," understood them, and, largely because of her age, physical characteristics, and general demeanor, imparted a warm and sympathetic concern for other people's problems.

The union's choice in assigning an organizer had been less fortunate in 1947. Betty was a much younger person — a woman in her mid-twenties. She had been raised and college trained in New York City, and she had had no experience as a worker in the industry.

This is not to suggest that Helen would have succeeded in 1947 or that Betty would have failed in 1950-51. There were obvious differences in the intensity of dissatisfaction and the number of workers affected by it. In addition, the general climate of opinion among the workers regarding the legitimacy of unions played an important part. The local labor movement in Saylor, which, for the most part, had been organized during World War II, was a few years older and considerably more experienced by 1950. During the postwar period, the mill workers had seen members of their families and their neighbors join unions, receive benefits, and not lose their jobs. There was less fear of employer reprisal in 1950 than there had been three years earlier. Further, the chief organizer himself had been fairly new to his job in 1947. By 1950 he had considerably more organizing experience and knew a good deal more about organizing methods. A careful survey of the organizing potential among the mill workers was undertaken in 1950, but not before in the earlier effort. If it had been made, perhaps the organizing effort would not have been attempted at that time.

Additional factors which lay outside the mill and even the community had an impact upon the situation. In 1947, the passage of the Taft-Hartley Act contributed to the responsible union official's decision to abandon an already difficult organizing campaign. By 1950 the general climate of opinion was such that the union organizers were no longer convinced that organizing drives in this part of the country were doomed to failure.

Whatever the factors, however, an organizer is not likely to succeed unless he adapts his tactics to the organizing situation. He must be able to emphasize that aspect of unionism which will attract the worker he is trying to convince. He must be able to judge when to work in secret and when to come out into the open. He must be able to deal effectively with a variety of individuals to whom unionism might mean quite different things. He must know when to proffer advice and when to admit lack of knowledge. He must know what resources he can call upon to help him in his task. Without imagination and flexibility, he probably will not be very successful. In sum, his tactics are determined by his assessment of the reasons workers may have for joining the union, the economic and cultural climate in which the organizing attempt is undertaken, and the kind of workers and company with whom he is dealing. The interplay of these factors largely accounts for differences in organizing tactics.

In Saylor the personal approach through home visits was not only feasible but also of great importance. As a result of the work setup, communication and personal contact had been at a minimum inside the mill. Most workers had only personal versions and explanations of their dissatisfactions, and these were generally vague and not crystallized as clear-cut and specific complaints. By playing the role of the sympathetic listener, Helen left it to the worker to define his dissatisfactions for himself. At the same time she strengthened the workers' feelings of security and need for justification by adjusting her approach to the fears, doubts, and experiences of each individual. It can be assumed that because the workers had the opportunity to talk at length to a sympathetic listener about their experiences, they probably became more aware of them, and their dissatisfactions were strengthened. In many cases they continued the discussion with members of their families, many of whom were union members, after Helen left. The personal approach had the additional advantage of enabling the organizer to assess constantly the prevailing sentiments, attitudes, and relationships in the mill as they developed on a day-to-day basis. Her sensitivity was increased correspondingly, and her interaction with workers was facilitated.

Discontent, however, did not lead the "fence-sitters" to join the union. It was largely cancelled out by a number of other factors operating in varying degrees of strength. These workers had little or no experience, either directly or indirectly, with unions. Accordingly, their images and expectations of a union as a problem-solving agency was extremely limited or nonexistent. It is important to note that the average age of the fence-sitters was significantly higher than that of the active union members. Similarly, on the average, the fence-sitters had been in the firm's employ for almost twice as long as the strikers. The proportion of primary wage-earners among the fence-sitters was high. When they realized that the employer was taking a hostile attitude toward unionism, they were loath to incur his displeasure and to risk losing their jobs, particularly in a community where there were few, if any, alternate work opportunities.

All of these factors, to varying degrees, contributed to the doubts and fears of the fence-sitters and, hence, to their confessed confusion. The influences from the union, on the one side, and from the employer on the other, coupled with their own insecurities, tended to induce them to remain neutral in a situation fraught with conflicting pressures. Although the active members tended to have similar doubts and fears, these were often outweighed by their perspective of "union" in terms of some ideology which permitted them to view it in a favorable light. This was clearly not the case among the fence-sitters, since for practically all of them the notion that a union could be useful in solving problems, including enhancing their security in the mill, was new and foreign. In this connection, it is interesting to note that the only worker in the leadership group who withdrew from the union at one time was, at the same time, the only member of that group whose dissatisfactions were not fortified with a union ideology of some kind. She had never had any prior experience with a union, either directly or indirectly.

For the fence-sitters, not joining the union meant being cut off from co-workers who had joined; joining implied taking great risks and, for some, being cut off from an employer whom they admired and respected. Lacking perspectives of their own, the fence-sitters tended to become more responsive to what others said and did; if one joined with initial reservations or became apprehensive and confused after joining, her sensitivity to the actions and sentiments of those close to her in the work group was increased. They tended to face their dilemma initially by hesitating to act at all. Then, when they acted, the move was predicated by a need to conform with the actions of those with whom they worked closest and knew best. Thus, those fence-sitters who joined early in the organizing drive tended to do so because others in their immediate work groups had joined. Similarly, if they withdrew subsequently, they tended to do so because others had withdrawn. And when they rejoined during the latter stages of the organizing drive or the strike, this action also was primarily predicated by their need to conform with the behavior of the majority of their co-workers.[6]

Although only a few non-joiners were interviewed, it appears significant that seventeen of them were concentrated in two departments of the mill. The organizers were unable to find any individuals in these two departments who were willing to assume leadership roles on behalf of the union. Since leadership roles in other departments were taken by individuals who had had previous union experience, it may be safe to assume that such experienced individuals were not present in the departments which remained non-union. Further, those who did not join were, on the average, both older and in the company's employ longer than the others. Again, the non-joiners represented the highest proportion of primary wage-earners in the mill, and some physically handicapped persons, whose income might have been cut off if they had been displaced because of joining the union, were in this group. The few younger workers who remained out of the union were either close relatives or friends of mill supervisors. Thus, it may be assumed that many of the same considerations which caused some workers to become fence-sitters obtained among the non-members.

It seems clear that the absence of individuals who would act as union missionaries, however motivated, may be sufficient to explain the failure of workers in a department to join a union. Indeed, it may be concluded that the presence within a group of workers of a single individual who identifies with an employer and who, at the same time, is able to influence the behavior of co-workers may be sufficient to induce others to stay out of a new union.

---

[6] "Conformity" is an old and well-established social-psychological concept. Allport, Newcomb, Sherif, Patrick and Simms, Stouffer, Shils, Roethlisberger and Dickson, Thrasher and Whyte have dealt with this concept in various settings. See Otto Klineberg, *Social Psychology* (New York, 1954), pp. 456-58.

From the very first, the organizers sought to lay a sound basis for group action. Only after there was sufficient evidence that some degree of group cohesiveness had developed could the campaign be brought into the open. While the organizer knew that the emphasis on secrecy gave a hesitant individual a sense of security, he also was certain that the news of union activity would spread rapidly through the mill. Increasing communication among workers not only contributed to a merging of individual dissatisfactions but also tended to give the individual a sense of collective support which, in turn, encouraged more and more workers to join the union.

In order to provide a symbol of opposition upon which to focus the causes of workers' grievances, the union organizer usually seeks to build up the employer as an "enemy" — the person to blame for unjust conditions. The presence of an "enemy" functions as a basis for further organizing the feelings of the new union members on behalf of the union and for fostering their attachment to the union — thus yielding greater solidarity.[7] An "enemy" symbol permits the organizer to sharpen his objectives and to loosen the workers' attachment to the employer. It further enables him to break down the workers' previous ways of viewing the causes of their complaints and to increase the possibility of action along the lines which he proposes.

This was a particularly difficult strategy to develop at Saylor. The employer had been a symbol of authority, prestige, and benevolence in the community. His family had enjoyed a favorable reputation over a period of many decades as a result of contributions to and general support of the Catholic church and was regarded by the mill

---

[7] The "enemy" represents an out-group in relation to the in-group of union members. Each group views itself as the upholder of virtue and justice and seeks to develop among its members feelings of loyalty and identification. "The out-group is regarded as unscrupulous and vicious and is felt to be attacking the values which the in-group holds dear. Before the out-group the members of the in-group not only feel that they are right and correct, but believe that they have a common responsibility to defend and preserve their values. The value of these in-group — out-group attitudes in developing solidarity . . . is quite clear. The belief on the part of its members that the movement is being opposed unjustly and unfairly by vicious and unscrupulous groups serves to rally the members around their aims and values. To have an enemy, in this sense, is very important for imparting solidarity to the movement. . . ." Herbert Blumer, "Collective Behavior," in *New Outlines of the Principles of Sociology*, p. 207. See also, Georg Simmel, *Conflict* (Glencoe, Ill., 1955), pp. 97-98.

employees with respect and even admiration. Thus, the usual technique of characterizing the employer as a "demon" could not be used. Phil related that he "worked under wraps" prior to the strike,

because I felt, and I think I was right, that a lot of people would resent any direct attack on Miller as a person, and I had to do it in a roundabout way to show that regardless of what kind of an individual Tom was, as an employer he's a son-of-a-bitch. But I never dared to express myself very strongly for fear that some people might take his side. . . . I never did attack him as an individual. At the early stages of the organizing, the people had such liking for him that it had to be the floorlady who was responsible, but Tom Miller had to be a good guy. I had to go along with this. Although I never said he was a good guy, I had to pull my punches. I used the easy way of referring to "The Company" and making it very clear that to me "The Company" was anyone who is a member of the corporation or in a supervisory capacity. I talked about an abstraction, "The Company." I never felt, before the strike, that I could attack him personally.

Indeed, the general referent, "The Company," did permit and encourage workers to relate their specific work dissatisfactions in any way they chose. For some workers, "The Company" was a forelady; for others, a foreman; for still others, the superintendent. For many, it was simply the generalized source of irritation about wages, hours, vacations, and other such matters. But, as we shall see in the next chapter, the "enemy" was not Tom Miller until after the strike began.

Phil's objective was to find ways to organize the feelings of the workers on behalf of the union and to forge a new social structure in the mill which would exclude the employer and his supervisory force. His primary tool was the "inside organizing committee." Workers who had responded most favorably to the organizer's appeal for unionization were singled out and assigned status in the new organization. They were given the specific task of feeling out fellow workers, arranging Helen's personal calls, and talking up the union in the shop. The almost daily meetings in Helen's hotel room brought them into intimate contact with each other and the professional organizer. They were no longer just workers in the mill; instead they were developing new self-conceptions as "union leaders" who communicated to their fellow workers the strategies of the professional organizers in building the union and negotiating a contract. Their activities were particularly important during the prolonged contract negotiations. It was primarily through this group that all events became communicated to co-workers. The in-plant leaders became instrumental in fostering common attitudes and in changing workers' definitions of the situation.[8]

Under the guidance of the organizers, the in-plant leaders appealed to groups of workers with different interests. On the one hand, the repeated emphasis upon the union's patience, good will, and tolerance appealed to those who were still suspicious of unionism and either sympathetic to or afraid of their employer. On the other hand, the hesitancy to call a strike increased tension and restlessness among those who, from the very beginning of organization, had shown greater willingness to fight for their demands. The union became a major topic of conversation in the mill, and the tensions of those who were urging a strike were communicated to others. As a result, the prestige of the union increased as that of the employer declined.

Still other techniques were used by the organizers, who recognized that many workers faced a conflict between their desires to improve shop conditions and their feelings or attachment to or fear of their employer. By contrasting their working conditions with those prevailing in other unionized sectors of the industry or the town and by laying the blame for their dissatisfactions primarily upon the supervisors or upon the abstract "Company," the organizers avoided direct criticism of the employer and minimized the possibility of antagonizing workers. By trying to divorce the employer's role as mill manager and owner from his other roles in the community, the organizers were able to characterize the company as the "enemy" without challenging the employer's integrity as a person.

Tom Miller's early and firm opposition to the union convinced Phil that the developing struggle would eventually involve not only

---

[8] The interaction between rank-and-file members and the in-plant leaders or organizers was exceedingly complex. It is not my intention to imply that a small number of persons created the group. Hiller points out that: "The leader usually symbolizes the group . . . if he does not initiate action ways which the members are prepared to follow, he loses dominance. He must either act as an agent in uniting individuals around some interest which they think is worth striving for, or solidify them around himself. He thus becomes a focus of attention, a collective representation." Ernest T. Hiller, *The Strike: A Study in Collective Action* (Chicago, 1928), p. 44.

the mill workers but others in the community as well. He suggested the United Labor Committee as a device for enlisting the support of other unionized workers. Leaders of the Saylor Trades and Labor Council and representatives of other unions came regularly to meetings of the mill workers. They repeatedly asserted their solidarity with and support of the mill workers and were instrumental in publicizing the union's claims throughout the community. The names of mill workers who crossed the picket line during the strike were posted on union bulletin boards in every plant and union office in the community. The regular appearance of other union members at the mill picket line gave both physical and moral support to the striking women.

The authority and prestige of the Catholic church was enlisted when a leaflet quoting a leading member of the church hierarchy was distributed to mill workers before the representation election. The frequent appearance of a local priest at strike headquarters clearly gave church support to the union and probably had an important influence upon the Catholic community in general.

In the face of all of these union activities, the employer sought to promote a group solidarity that would include everyone associated with the enterprise except the union organizers whom he constantly characterized as outsiders. Like the union organizers, Tom Miller tried to justify himself and discredit his opponent. He minimized the extent of the workers' grievances by absolving himself from knowledge of their existence and proclaiming that he was prepared, as always, to deal privately with individual employees. He appealed to the community sentiment of the workers by posing as the guardian of their interests both in and out of the mill. He attempted to capitalize on the stereotype of the labor organizer: "professional promoter," "ambitious outsider," "stranger," and the like, whose primary interest was in extorting money in the form of union dues and assessments from gullible workers. He tried to give his employees the impression that the organizers were "crooks" or exploiters who preferred to live by their wits rather than to earn an "honest" living. In short, he, no less than the union organizers, attempted to construct an in-group which would exclude the union and its representatives.

Although he had always acted as a benefactor of his employees and was regarded by many of them as a person of esteem and of benevolence, he chose to oppose the wishes of the majority of his employees as demonstrated in a government-supervised election. Thus the basically conflicting logics of employer and employees came to the fore. The logic by which Tom Miller operated told him that as manager and controller of a business enterprise, his duty was to retain maximum control of the business apparatus and the freedom to maximize business profit. The intervention of the union directly challenged this logic. If the union were organized, he felt that the workers, through their union, would wrest from him large areas of decision-making authority. There is no question but that he was serious and conscientious in his concern for the welfare of his employees, but according to his logic, he was the legitimate guardian of their welfare in the mill and his authority should be respected and obeyed.

The logic of his employees, however, was quite different. They sought to protect existing rights and to secure new gains in the light of ever developing new conceptions of what constituted their rights and dues as employees. They did not expect a man who had a reputation as a benevolent patriarch to oppose their expressed intentions to form a union. When Tom Miller made it clear that he would not cooperate with his workers in carrying out their mandate to get a union contract, he convinced many still hesitant workers that he was not really concerned about what they wanted. Many came to feel that he no longer was to be trusted and no longer deserved their loyalty. In opposing the demonstrated wishes of a majority of his employees, he convinced many of them that he no longer was their friend but was just an employer.

Tom Miller used two features of the Taft-Hartley Act to great advantage in his efforts to combat union organization. The first was the slow-moving and cumbersome machinery of the National Labor Relations Board which administers the Act. The various levels of Board organization permit appeals from the decisions of subordinates to higher authority, and this takes time. A chronology of Board activities in the mill case gives some indication of the time-consuming process.

The union filed the original petition for a representation election in mid-September, 1950, and the election was held on October 24. Two days after the union's victory was announced, the company filed an objection, contesting the conduct of the election, with the NLRB regional office. The regional director denied the company's objection in mid-December. On December 26, the company appealed to the National Board. Two months went by before the NLRB ruled against the company. A week later, on February 27, the company filed a motion asking the Board to reconsider its earlier decision. On March 28, 1951, the Board denied the motion to reconsider. Thus, more than seven months passed between the time the union first filed its petition for an election and the election results were finally certified. During this period, the proportion of union supporters among the mill workers dropped from 90 per cent to a little more than 50 per cent, and the strength of union conviction of at least part of the remaining members could be seriously questioned.

The second feature of the Act used extensively by Miller in his opposition to the union was the "free speech" provision. Section 8(c) states that the expression of views or opinions by an employer is not an unfair labor practice so long as it does not contain a threat of reprisal or force or promise of benefit. The NLRB had ruled a "captive audience" meeting was a protected activity under this section, and Miller used such meetings liberally in expressing his opposition to the union. Further, many of the letters which he sent to his employees contained odious references to the union and its representatives, and these, also, would undoubtedly have been considered as protected free speech under the law.

It is important to note here that the Act proclaims it to be the policy of the United States to encourage collective bargaining by "protecting the exercise by workers of full freedom of association, self-organization, and designation of representatives of their own choosing, for the purpose of negotiating the terms and conditions of their employment or other mutual aid or protection."[9]

Yet Miller's tactics had a notable effect upon the workers' "full freedom" with respect to joining the union. Although neither the captive audience speeches nor the letters contained any clear threats of reprisal or promises of benefit, they made it perfectly clear to the workers that their employer strongly disapproved of their union mem-

[9] U. S. Congress, *Labor-Management Relations Act, 1947*, Public Law 101, 80th Cong., 1st Sess., 1947, Sec. 101, sub-sec. 1.

bership. In the Saylor situation, where few alternate employment opportunities existed, Tom Miller's words probably carried greater weight than they might have in other situations. Many workers viewed his statements as veiled threats of reprisal — loss of job or discriminatory treatment should the unionizing effort fail. They were considered intimidating and coercive — far more than simply an expression of his views. The statements, coupled with his sponsorship of petitions to withdraw from the union, further restricted the workers' freedom to exercise their rights under the law.

The union might have had grounds for bringing unfair labor practice charges before the NLRB on the supervisors' roles in circulating membership-withdrawal petitions and on the wage increase which was given unilaterally while the employer's appeal was pending before the Board. But the organizers deliberately chose not to seek recourse through the Board's machinery since such a move would have produced even greater delays during which the effects of the employer's anti-union campaign would have increased.

Tom Miller's use of the Act made an initially difficult organizing campaign even more difficult. His strategy of using every appeal opportunity within the cumbersome NLRB machinery and, at the same time, sponsoring activities designed to undermine the employees' interest in unionism paid off large dividends. His granting of a unilateral wage increase, holding captive audience meetings, sending letters to employees, and sponsoring petitions to withdraw from union membership succeeded very effectively in cutting down the union's majority until it all but disappeared.

Phil was faced with substantial problems in countering Tom Miller's strategy. It was always part of his own strategy to involve as many workers as possible in the union's activities. But if morale was to be maintained at a high level, the union and their activities in it had to produce some positive results. More than anything else, Phil felt that he had to show the workers that the union was doing all in its power to bring the conflict to an end, and this meant that he had to "keep things moving" at all times. He had to convince the workers that in spite of the long delays and the union's apparent inactivity, the union really "was not standing still." In spite of all his efforts, many members clearly came to feel that it was.

One of the tests of the resourcefulness of an organizer is his ability to deal with this problem. Since there could be no progress in settling any collective bargaining issues until bargaining had begun, and since bargaining would not begin until the government agency had finally certified the union, the organizers kept things moving by setting up a host of social activities in which the workers could participate as union members — picnics, parties, dances, small and close meetings in Helen's hotel room, breakfast and dinner meetings, and movies on trade union subjects.

But Phil used other and perhaps more important tactics. He responded in kind to each letter Tom Miller sent to the workers. When the employer held a captive audience meeting, the union answered either by sending a personal letter to the workers or by holding a special meeting in the union hall. When the petitions for withdrawal were circulated, the organizers stepped up personal contacts either by house calls or small group meetings. As the employer's counteroffensive gained momentum, Phil brought in top union officials to speak at large membership meetings. Phil made a deliberate effort to counter Mr. Miller's moves one by one, as they occurred. These things were not planned in advance. The union's tactics were forged on a day-by-day, sometimes even an hour-by-hour, basis. Phil had to do all he could to convince the new union members that the union was not, as several leaders felt, "letting grass grow under its feet."

The claims and counterclaims of the union and the employer are part of the tactical efforts of interests in conflict to influence the behavior of workers. The confusion and indecision which many workers expressed can be explained as largely the result of these claims and counterclaims. In this kind of situation, the opinions and actions of fellow workers who are "prestigeful" in the shop society become crucial.

In events and processes such as those reported here, the role of the professional union organizer who is backed by the resources of a powerful institution is critical and may be decisive. He comes to symbolize the group, and in a democratic society his leadership will be accepted and maintained only so long as he initiates actions which his membership is prepared to follow. He acts as an agent in uniting individuals around some common goal which they may be seeking, or he may try to unite them around himself. He becomes a focus of attention and a collective representation which articulates the hopes and fears of his followers.

There are times and situations when even the most resourceful organizer will not succeed. At other times and in different situations no professional organizer is needed. It seems reasonably clear that the organizing environment of the mid-1930's no longer exists in any part of the United States, and there is no reason to assume that it will return. The large potential for union growth — the newly industrialized South, the white-collar and professional occupations, government and farm workers, and the increasingly scattered and decentralized industry of the North — presents difficult organizing problems. Methods and techniques which proved successful in 1935 are not likely to achieve the same kind of results in 1958. In the absence of mass unrest among vast sections of the union membership potential, the act of joining a union is much more likely to be perceived by the worker as a far more personal thing than it was during periods when millions of workers flocked into unions faster than the organizations could accommodate them. In the new environment, the professional organizer becomes the key person.

He is not likely to succeed unless he adapts his tactics to the organizing situation. A method which he has used successfully in one situation may fail completely in another. The professional organizer acts on the basis of certain general principles which are differentially applied as the people, the industry, the time, and the place indicate. He is a pragmatist operating in a world characterized by power and struggles for power. He employs few, if any, ironclad rules. He is measured and judged according to the successes and failures which he records. His role is best described in the words of the leading actor in the Saylor events:

I organized a union and I ran a strike. When you have a job to do, you do it. If anyone tells you that there's a fixed way of running a strike, that you can plan it, they're insane. You build it from day to day, just like you build a union from day to day. There's nothing you can plan ahead. Sure, you can plan pickets, you can plan picket signs and songs, you can plan a kitchen and benefits. But your behavior, it varies from moment to moment according to the needs of the situation, and the important thing is to be there and be ready to do it, whatever it is, and go ahead and do it.

7

Why the Strike—
An Analysis of the Workers' Views

The Saylor company workers held various opinions about the legitimacy of the strike weapon and its application to their situation. Many of them expressed reservations about strikes in general — usually on the grounds that strikes "need not be" since alternative and peaceful means for settling union-management disputes exist or should exist.

But none of the union leaders disapproved of their own strike.[1] They were convinced that their employer was unwilling to come to an amicable settlement with the union. Therefore, they felt that they had only two choices: to strike or to abandon any hope of organizing a union. Once having chosen to oppose the employer by joining a union, they had made an irrevocable commitment to themselves and to their co-workers. To strike became their only feasible course of action, since to abandon the union would have left many of them with no protection from the employer whom they had defied. They could only hope that the strike movement would be successful and that the union would protect them from the employer's recriminations. Local leaders in particular held this view.

Once the chips were down and we saw that we couldn't get anything

---

[1] It is important to remember that the interviews were taken after the strike ended in a claimed union victory. It is not unlikely that a different view might have been obtained if the outcome had been different.

any other way and once we were out, we knew that we had to win. There was no losing it. Most of the fellows said they'd never go back to work there if we lost. Once you're in a thing like that, you have to go all out if you want to win, and you have to win. You can't turn back.

One leader added that a strike was the only language the employer could understand:

The negotiations looked like an endless struggle and we had no alternative but to go on strike. It was our only weapon. Everybody felt that it had to be. Many of the others wanted it a lot earlier, right after the certification election when it began to look like Tom Miller was stalling us. We felt that a strike was the only way we could deal with Miller.

The company's move to delay dealing with the union by appealing its case to the highest level of the National Labor Relations Board convinced the workers that their employer was deliberately erecting obstacles to thwart their desires. They felt that only a strike would show the employer that his workers could not be rebuffed.

I was for it. I thought it was necessary because we wouldn't have gotten anywhere without it. It was the only way to show Miller that we meant business. Where could you get without a strike in such a situation? Nowhere!

In addition, the leaders were convinced that not only was the employer responsible for the strike but that he also was responsible for creating the kind of sentiment among the workers which made the strike inevitable.

I was for it because we had tried everything else and we were all in a fighting mood. Tom got us in that mood. We were disgusted about the delays, and we were determined that we should not be without a union.

Although none of the rank-and-file union members was clearly opposed to the strike, many held reservations. Their feelings were that a strike was not something to be undertaken in a casual way. It involved serious considerations and considerable risk. It was forced upon the workers, they felt, and was undertaken only as a final resort. A woman striker, who had been employed in the mill for more than twenty-five years, expressed her initial reservations:

I was for it, but at the same time I didn't feel good about it. I had worked there so long, and I felt it wasn't right to strike. The company had been very nice to me, and sometimes when I didn't feel well, they would let me come to work any time I felt like it and I appreciated that. But I felt we had to strike. We just weren't treated right in a lot of ways. I voted for the strike in the end.

Many feared the economic power of the employer:

I was a little reluctant at first because I didn't know if we would ever get a contract that way because the Millers are a tough proposition to be up against. I didn't think Tom Miller would ever give in, especially if we went on strike. But then I felt that if we didn't get a contract to protect us, after going so far, we'd all be let out one by one, and we'd never get a job in this town again because of the influence the Millers have here. We would all be marked people.

A striker, whose husband was active in his union in another establishment, felt that the strike was long overdue but that the employer represented a formidable opponent. "I felt that this was something that should have happened years before. But nobody had the gumption to battle with the Millers."

The majority of the rank-and-file members asserted that they voted for and supported the strike move largely because others did. They only vaguely understood and accepted the idea of the strike as a legitimate union weapon. Indeed, they understood and accepted the specific contract demands of their union only in the most general terms. However, they faced a paramount need to conform with the behavior of co-workers and leaders whose opinions carried the most prestige and whose anticipated judgments of themselves counted the most. One such worker had had some prior experience with strikes in another city.

I was sick about [the mill strike] when it started. I saw and heard about strikes in Milwaukee, and I was scared. Those were real battles and cars got turned over and people got badly hurt. But I thought that the union would make things better all the way around here, and if we had to strike for a union in the mill, I was scared but willing to go with the rest of the girls.

Often a worker would justify the strike by pointing to the absence of alternatives. Then he would add: "Everybody else seemed to be in favor of it and wanted to strike, and I wanted to stick with them." This influence of the group upon the individual had a strong impact upon the fence-sitters as well as upon the rank-and-file members. The fence-sitters had joined the union with reservations and, for the most part, had the same reservations about the strike.

When the strike began, I wanted to be with the greater majority of the people. I realized that if the people all pulled together, we could win, and then there wouldn't be so much discord in the mill as there was before the union came in.

Workers who held this view (and there were many) were saying, implicitly, that out of conflict would come a new social structure which would eliminate the tensions of the shop society.

Several of the fence-sitters came to the mill expecting to go to work the first day of the strike. The determination of their co-workers on the picket line deterred them and later induced them to join the union. The issues in the dispute were either not understood or not considered relevant to their immediate situation. But the behavior of their co-workers was.

The first day of the strike I just stood around and watched. Then I went home and thought for a long while. When I saw all the girls out there and how determined they were, I thought that the only thing to do was to join and be with them.

THE PICKETING

Although there are strikes without picket lines and picket lines without strikes, the two weapons of labor so often go together that they are frequently considered part of the same general phenomenon. The appearance of a picket line around an industrial plant or a business establishment may often be the first public indication of a labor dispute.

Picketing is difficult to define because its purpose or aim is not always the same. Apparently the most legally acceptable form of picketing is illustrated by one or two persons walking back and forth in front of an establishment and carrying placards proclaiming that a strike is in progress or that the employer is "unfair" to organized labor in some specific respect. Such a picket line is designed to be informative, and the potential customer or the worker is left to draw his own conclusions. It is designed to be persuasive, urging support of often unspecified demands of the labor organization.

"Peaceful" picketing depends upon the support of those toward whom it is directed. However, frequently unions enjoy no sympathy either from the buying public or from other workers. To meet this difficulty, a union may attempt other types of picketing, the aims of which are less persuasive than coercive. If management makes no attempt to operate a struck plant, picketing may be a mere formality or may even be dispensed with completely. But if the union anticipates that the employer will seek to operate the struck enterprise, picketing takes on the character of a major tactical weapon. It is organized to exercise a moral and physical deterrent upon those who want to get into the plant to carry on production.

A union may attempt, by picketing, to completely isolate a firm economically by stopping shipments into or out of the establishment. Thus, cars and trucks may be halted and searched for what the pickets consider to be contraband. Pickets also may attempt to prevent trains from entering or leaving the struck premises.

A picket line which operates in this fashion actually attempts to enforce a blockade in a war of attrition against the struck firm. If the picket line is attacked by those who would seek to cross it, it may become a symbol of the struggle between the union members and the firm, and the strikers may fight to protect it. In this kind of situation, the substantive issues which produced the strike may become submerged or even forgotten in the effort to protect or attack the picket line. This actually happened in Saylor.

From the first day of the strike until its conclusion, the picket line functioned as the major deterrent to mill workers who had not joined the strike. The appearance of the "scabs" was a new experience for the vast majority of the strikers. Only a few of the local leaders had ever heard the term before, and only a few of the strikers had any notion of the function of a picket line.

The calling of the strike created much excitement and tension, since none of the union members knew quite what to anticipate. Phil told them that a picket line would be organized, but only a few of them could imagine what it was supposed to do. As yet, there were no established rules for the pickets and no codes of behavior. When the picket line was attacked by the Mayor and police on the first day of the strike, the incipient excitement and tension became focused upon the non-strikers, and mechanisms related to crowd behavior were generated.[2] The pickets resisted the Mayor and police by acting

---
[2] L. L. Bernard, "Crowd," *Encyclopedia of Social Sciences,* IV, pp. 612-13;

on the basis of aroused impulses rather than established rules. Individuals who later regarded their own behavior as non-permissible acted on the picket line with the assured feelings that they were part of a group and that the group behavior was permissible. Many strikers were amazed to see some of the quietest of their co-workers suddenly emerge as the most aggressive on the picket line.

For the women, the picketing experience was unique in other ways. Not only had they never before engaged in such behavior, but they also suddenly found themselves the center of attention in Saylor. Daily routines of their otherwise obscure lives were dramatically interrupted, and they became the object and subject of considerable attention all over town. A local high school teacher said that the spectacle of women strikers and the things they did were important factors in winning over a large segment of community support to the strikers' cause:

You have to realize what it means in this community when the circus or a carnival comes to town. It's a major event of the year. The strike was here for sixteen weeks and something new was happening every day, something different. Hundreds of the local citizens gathered almost every day across the street from the plant and watched the pickets who were very creative and imaginative in attracting attention to their cause. The strike was a constant subject of conversation all over town — at bridge clubs and poker clubs and at the supper tables. People were always going around and asking each other if they knew what happened at the mill today. I suppose that most of the stories that were told were myths and fiction. But there were stories continually being told — truth or fiction, and it was a constant source of conversation. The women used all kinds of tricks and it became a big show for the local citizenry; the mirrors and the smudge barrels and the banging on the saws and the ridiculous things that Miller did to retaliate. He hung curtains over the windows and then painted the windows, and the lengths he went to get coal in — even tried to bring it in by parcel post. There was always something going on there which was a feature attraction for the community.

Thus, the pickets and the strike were topics of conversation throughout the community; the Mayor had sought the strikers out for special attention, as had the Chief of Police and the County Sheriff. Strikers'

Gustave LeBon, *The Crowd: A Study of the Popular Mind* (London, 1897); Park and Burgess, Chs. XII and XIII.

pictures and many articles describing their activities on the picket line were published in the newspaper.

As a result of their experiences the first day of the strike, reinforced by Phil's continuing leadership, the strikers developed the belief that picketing was absolutely necessary if their strike was to be a success. When the picket line was attacked not only by the employer but also by the town's chief law enforcement officers, the strike took on a new dimension. From that point on, the city administration became identified with the employer in the strikers' minds, and their determination was greatly increased.

During the later stages of the strike, when the pickets' morale tended to sag, the organizer could refer to the incidents and successes of the first day. Phil would point out that if the strikers' determination could stop the leading officials of Saylor, continued determination would bring the employer to his knees. "We formed a wall of flesh to keep the Mayor and the police and the scabs out," one worker said. "If we can do that, we knew we could eventually beat the Millers." After the first day, there was little that the organizers could tell the pickets about their duties; they had learned by experience what it meant to picket in the face of determined efforts by non-strikers to enter the plant.

We were all green at it at first, but we learned and we learned quick. I certainly did picket, and even though I was scared at first and didn't know what to do, we saw that it had to be done. The scabs had to be given a hard time.

As a result of the initial incidents of violence, the strikers developed a belief that the picketing was justified on the ground that it was a defense tactic and not alone or even primarily a tactic designed to win collective bargaining demands. The immediate issues that separated the union from the employer were completely submerged. The picket line became a symbol of the entire effort. "We never missed a day. We were fighting for our rights on the picket line," many strikers said. Members of the strike committee in particular saw their new duties as vital to the outcome of the strike. They were the appointed lieutenants of the professional organizers, and they had been singled out to be given new roles.

I picketed constantly. I practically lived there. I was determined to win. It was my job, and I felt as much concerned about the picketing as I did about my job when I was working. In fact, I put in a lot of time on the line that I'd never put in at my job.

The pickets emphasized that their picketing was a diversion from the normal routine of daily life, both inside and outside the mill. They often pointed to the devices which they invented to harass and embarrass the "scabs":

We made the picket line a lot of fun. We did all sorts of things — you've heard about the noisemakers and the mirrors and the barrels of tar. We made dummies of the scabs and the bosses and hung them on the poles around the factory. We came down in costumes and we sang all sorts of songs and had parties. It got so we couldn't stay away from the picket line for fear we'd miss some fun. We actually made fun out of a grim struggle.

And, indeed, "making fun out of a grim struggle" contributed much to the morale and perseverance of the strikers. Picket line duty was generally preferred to work in the strike kitchen because "more exciting things happened there. . . . It was lots of fun."

Several of the strikers pointed out that the picket line gave them an opportunity to know their co-workers more intimately.

It was fun after a while, and you really got to know the people you used to work with but maybe never knew them more than to say "hello." We saw them every day and really got to know them.

This striker was really saying that the picket line, more than anything else, brought the workers together and made a social group out of a disparate amalgam of semi-isolated individuals. And as a group, the strikers became the focus of attention in the community. "I met different cops and deputies and now I know them all. We drew a crowd every night." Many of the strikers who held initial reservations about picketing later modified their views to wholehearted support of the picket line after it had attracted so much general attention and had proven to be so successful. At first some of them picketed only because their co-workers were doing so. Later they adopted a different view of the picket role:

I thought I might just as well picket to show our people that I was in it all the way. And if too many of them stayed home, what was the sense of the strike? After we were on the line a few days, we were afraid to miss a day because we didn't want to miss any of the excitement. I'm not sorry I picketed. We had lots of fun. We saw the reaction of the scabs about the strike and the bosses, too. I think all of us that were on the line stayed there because we were afraid we'd miss something. Even my husband came down all the time, and he didn't know what to do with himself evenings when it was all over.

Notice that this striker, like so many others, used the group referent "we" when talking about the picket line activity. For her, as for the others on the line, it was the group which was the unit of action, not the individual. A group solidarity had developed to submerge the identity of the individual striker.

The fence-sitters did not share these experiences since, with few exceptions, they worked in the strike headquarters kitchen. Typically, they objected to the conduct of the pickets and the violence which occurred.

If there's something I wouldn't like to do, it's picketing. It's too rough for me — too rowdy. They had some rowdy people there and they'd say things that were embarrassing. It wasn't coming to some of them that worked regardless of whether they go into the mill or not. God, the language used! It was awful, and it all went right into the papers. Some got much too radical.

Several of the fence-sitters who had withdrawn earlier from the union sat out most of the strike at home, refusing either to identify openly with the strikers or to cross the picket line. Typically, they rejoined the union during the later stages of the strike when they became convinced that the union would win.

I went to work the day it started, and then I saw the strike was on. I went right home when I saw the girls fighting. I really wanted to be with the girls out there and I wouldn't go through the picket line. But I didn't picket either. I just didn't want to hang around there. You know, you really had to do things on the picket line that you wouldn't otherwise do. You really can't be as nice as you are and you must be mean and hateful — like soldiers in a battle.

Her circle of close friends, whose opinions of herself she most regarded, did not include mill workers. "My friends wouldn't have liked it if I stand out there and do things like that," she continued.

Other fence-sitters, as well as strikers, respected the picket line largely because of the influence of relatives who were union members. I didn't want to go through the picket line. I never tried to go in during the strike. I was ashamed to go in. I didn't want to be called a scab and I just stayed out — stayed home. My husband and son are both union men, and it would have been terrible if I went in to scab. So I just kept away.

She rejoined the union midway through the strike and then worked in the kitchen. "When I joined I told them that I would do anything they wanted me to, but I wouldn't go on the picket line. I'm too old to do things like that."

Only a few of the fence-sitters said they might have worked during the strike if the picket line had not deterred them physically.

I tried to go the first day, and the pickets wouldn't let me. There were some people there from different plants and they called me terrible names — like fat slob — and some man grabbed my arm. They had no right to touch me. That wasn't right.

An elderly worker who supported a disabled husband refused, like other fence-sitters, to come near the mill all through the strike, although she joined the union immediately after it was over.

I stayed home because I was caught in the middle. Mr. Draper and Eileen [a local leader] came around and talked to me every once in a while. They asked me not to strikebreak. They said they'd settle it fast if everybody would stay out. So I stayed out, and every week somebody would come over and talk to me. I was worried about the mill closing down, but Mr. Draper assured me that that wouldn't happen. I really didn't know what to do. Every week I kept on hoping and praying that it would be the last week. But I didn't try to go into the mill again. They were doing so many bad things — using shotguns and name-calling against those that worked. I didn't want to get into something like that. But it was hard. My husband has been sick and we didn't have much money. The money was going and it looked bad for us. But Mr. Draper gave me enough to take care of the bare necessities. You know, I was all mixed up because I remembered the Miller family as wonderful people. Mr. Miller called me several times and asked me to come in to work. But I had those girls to work alongside of when the strike was settled, and they wouldn't feel friendly toward me. I'd rather be on the friendly side with the girls. When Mr. Miller called, I told him that my nerves wouldn't take it. I kept on telling him and the union the same answer — I was in the middle of the road. My son-in-law was for the union. He kept on telling me not to go in. And my sister begged me not to join the union because she worked in the Millers' Department Store. As I said, I was in the middle of the road.

Many of the fence-sitters, themselves marginal union members, sympathized with the non-strikers in their efforts to work.

I just wouldn't picket. I just couldn't see myself picket because I believe that anybody who wanted to go in had just as much right as those who wanted to stay out. I wouldn't even go on the picket line to see what went on.

But even those who objected to the picketing and worked in the kitchen became involved in and identified with the union through their activity. "You learned a lot," a sixty-year-old fence-sitter said. "Like setting up a kitchen and feeding all those people and their families. The union did a good thing by that. We never saw anything like that around here before."

The reaction of one worker was interesting. She was an enthusiastic union member and strike supporter, but she shifted from the picket line to the kitchen as violence increased. A member of the Seventh-Day Adventist church, she opposed the violence on religious grounds. Yet she justified its use by others as the only way by which the non-strikers could be dissuaded from entering the mill.

I don't believe in violence, so I went into the kitchen after it started. I think it was all right as a whole though. Sometimes they got a little too violent, but so did the other side and it was always our people who would end up in the hospital. Even the Mayor couldn't come in, and that's the way they held the line. A wall of human flesh. Before they got that injunction, nobody could go through.

The picket line and the violence which occurred when it was attacked became the basis for a new orientation which tended to unify the strikers. Defense of the strike meant defense of the picket line, and the issues which separated the employer from the union became submerged. With the appearance of the non-strikers, a common symbol of the employer's opposition developed, and the bonds of organization and group identity increased among the strikers as the pickets showed their determination to resist the "scabs." Intense interaction on the picket line involved many hesitant workers emotionally and drew them into the ranks of the strikers. Those who went to the plant "just to see what was going on" found themselves in a situation which no longer lent itself to conflicting judgments about "right" and "wrong." A picket captain described the first days on the line:

The people that came out on the picket line, people who you felt would never do a thing like that, throw stones or pound on the big circular saws we had set up as noisemakers. The women had more guts than the men. The scabs were really aggravating them. The scabs would go in with smirks on their faces and were taking the people's jobs away — working at jobs that they never did before and didn't belong to them. The girls really got mad and acted on the spur of the moment. They did all kinds of things I never thought they would do.

Under the influence of the organizers, the concept "scabbing," became amplified and defined; it became the symbol for "traitor" and "thief," and it was enlarged to include a criticism of an employer who would encourage such activity. The presence of the non-strikers was used by many workers as a justification for the continuation of the strike and the violence.

The crowds, mass meetings, and protest slogans contributed greatly to the formation of the new social group and to a group or "we" consciousness. In the course of these activities, more and more workers were drawn into the orbit of influence of the already determined leaders of the group. The daily effort to keep the non-strikers out of the mill repeatedly stirred up feelings and maintained intense intercommunication among the strikers. With only few exceptions, the union members, including many of those who earlier had been hesitant to turn against the employer, focused their resentment upon the non-strikers. And for the women, especially, the picket line experience was unique. Routines of their daily lives had been dramatically interrupted, and they were encouraged to persist in their new behavior when they found themselves the most talked about and publicized group in the community.

None of this was surprising to the leaders of the international union. In a situation where conflict was latent, violence could be expected. This view was clearly expressed by the union vice-president who, commenting on the picket line violence, said: "What else could you expect in a war which is what a strike is? What do you expect the pickets to do — walk on the line with flowers for the scabs?" And, indeed, the pickets had no flowers.

The strike of the mill workers must be viewed first and foremost as a group activity. It was more than individual workers leaving their jobs, and it was more than the simple sum of workers' individual motivations before the strike. It was a complex activity in which different persons engaged according to their identification with other persons in the in-plant society. The new conceptions of what was "right" and what was "due" emerged as shared conceptions, as group definitions. The workers were held together by the unifying orientation of the abstract "union" and its agents, their own in-plant leaders.

Most of the workers approached the strike with only very generalized views of the union, its demands, and the legitimacy of the strike as a tactical weapon. These were essentially new and foreign ideas. The strike itself was viewed, at first, with much apprehension and many serious misgivings by all but the leaders. But with the apparent willingness of the in-plant leaders to strike, reinforced by the trusted official agent of the "union," the strike became an acceptable idea.

In the course of the organizing drive, workers in the various separate departments of the mill came to know each other as union members and formed new groups, led by the organizing committee members in each department. Having consciously accepted and retained union membership, they also accepted in a general way the dimly understood goals and values which that institution and its leaders advanced. Within the vague context of the union, they developed a measure of identification with fellow workers as union members. They were ready to acknowledge the legitimacy of the union's collective bargaining demands since these demands were put forward and supported by members of the in-plant organizing committee who were, at the same time, leaders of the in-plant social groups. Even though the specifics of the demands and, therefore, of the substantive issues of the strike were vague to all but the leaders, the demands and the strike were acceptable to the union members because they were advanced within the generalized context of "union" and were recommended by the leaders who were now its official agents.

The union members did not interpret their strike solely or even mainly as an attack upon their employer. The vague and generalized idea of "union" required a commitment by the individual to his coworkers and to a leader whom he trusted and respected as the official representative of the "union." For most workers, there could be no withdrawal of this commitment as long as their fellow workers, members of their own primary work group, did not similarly withdraw. Even though they still respected and even admired their employer, he was neither a member of a work group nor a member of the new generalized in-plant society — the larger "union" group. The anticipated consequences of their behavior toward him mattered less than the anticipated opinions of close friends and co-workers who were members of common and overlapping work groups in the shop society. Once they had committed themselves to others whose judgments of them were most important, to refuse to strike would have meant to desert co-workers, and for most, this had greater potential consequences than to desert the employer. Once membership in a new in-plant work group was firmly established around the generalized goal of the union, the mutual claims and expectations of the group members produced substantial informal pressure to go all the way.[3]

Although we have no conclusive evidence to support this inference, it is conceivable that the widespread support of the strike was initially more apparent than real. Relatively few workers were consciously aware of the substantive issues which separated the union from the employer. The large majority understood very well that there were numerous reasons for their dissatisfactions with their employer and their jobs. But the specifics of these dissatisfactions were personal matters, generally between the worker and his immediate supervisor or the worker and the immediate conditions of the job. The dis-

---

[3] The data presented by Stouffer and his associates in their study of *The American Soldier* supports the rather complex hypothesis that primary group solidarity functions in the corporate body to strengthen the motivations for the fulfillment of substantive prescriptions and commands issued by the official agents of the corporate body, within the context of a set of generalized morale predispositions or sense of obligation, in this case to the United States and its goals in the war. The latter need not be strongly present in consciousness but the legitimacy of its demands in numerous particular situations must exist. See Samuel A. Stouffer, *et al., The American Soldier* (Princeton, 1949), especially II, pp. 130-68. Shils further concludes from the Stouffer study that "the evidence does not support the hypothesis that devotion to patriotic ideals directly played a great part in the motivation of the soldiers. . . . Most of the soldiers attributed a relatively low order of efficacy to patriotic or political ideals in their assessment of their own experiences under fire." "Primary Groups in the American Army," *Continuities in Social Research,* p. 23.

satisfactions had become shared during the organizing drive but, again, in a general way within the context of the union and the work group. They were still personal matters to the individual workers or groups of workers in their separate departments. The union represented the general unifying structure and symbol for the many individual or work-group dissatisfactions, and its demands were the generalized demands of an organization representing the larger corporate body of union members.

Very few members, other than the leaders, had a clear-cut definition of the situation which could guide their behavior. For example, the strike vote at the membership meeting came as a surprise to all but the local leaders who had participated in the negotiations. The possibility of a strike had been discussed by rank-and-file members in the mill, but the organizers had gambled on a settlement without a strike. Further, the collapse in the negotiations came quite suddenly and there was no time to systematically develop sentiment for the strike. Members came to the meeting without knowing how they would vote, at least in part because they didn't know precisely what they would be asked to vote to do.

In a situation of this kind, the collective bargaining issues may be neither understood nor considered crucial. The acts of others whose opinions and judgments are considered to be most important may become the basis for a person's own behavior.[4]

It is possible that a majority of those who voted for the strike did so largely because they *assumed* that others would do the same without actually *knowing* that they would. The anticipated, although

---

[4] Cf. George Herbert Mead, *Mind, Self and Society* (Chicago, 1934), p. 138: "The individual experiences himself as such, not directly, but only indirectly, from the particular standpoint of other individual members of the same group, or from the generalized standpoint of the social group as a whole to which he belongs." In this formulation and in numerous others like it, Mead in effect advances the hypothesis that it is the groups of which the individual is a member that yield the significant frame of reference for self-evaluation. A number of writers have since developed this general hypothesis: cf. Muzafer Sherif, *Group Relations at the Crossroads* (New York, 1953); Robert K. Merton and Alice S. Kitt, "Contributions to the Theory of Reference Group Behavior," in Merton and Lazarsfeld, *op. cit.*; Theodore Newcombe, *Social Psychology* (New York, 1950); Herbert H. Hyman, "The Relation of the Reference Group to the Judgment of Status," in *The Psychology of Status*, Archives of Psychology, No. 269 (1942); Leon Festinger, "The Role of Group Belongingness in a Voting Situation," *Human Relations,* II (1947), 154-80.

unknown, behavior of co-workers may have been the important consideration. Thus, the initial support of the strike can be interpreted not so much as support for the union as response to a need to conform with the anticipated or imputed acts of friends and co-workers.

With each worker assuming that the others favored the strike — and with the opinions of those "significant others" being most important — a vote for the strike may be seen as a social act and may have had little or nothing to do with the larger union-management conflict. This suggests that the explanations most often given for why workers strike — generally grounded on economic considerations — may be only partial explanations going to the sources of dissatisfactions. Such explanations may have little relationship to the social reality of the strike itself.

Those who crossed the picket line to work had made no firm commitment about the union either to themselves or to their co-workers. They had not yet been drawn into the web of group affiliation and identification as had the union members. Until the strike occurred, they were still socially isolated in the plant society, although, as will be shown in the next chapter, they too developed a powerful group identification during the course of the strike. Concentrated as they were in two departments of the mill, their own closest associates, their own "significant others," were fellow workers who also stayed out of the union.

The fence-sitters, on the other hand, were caught in a highly ambiguous situation which lacked definition for them. They were, for the most part, older than the pickets and more dependent upon the employer for continued income. Many of them went into the kitchen because they abhorred the violence and because they conceived of themselves as "too old" to assume the new roles as pickets. Others, unable to define clearly their relationship to some co-workers who picketed and others who worked, resolved their role conflict either by working in the kitchen or by trying to disassociate themselves from the conflict by staying at home.

Just as the strike was interpreted differently by different workers, so also was the picketing and particularly the violence. Those who had made the firmest commitment to the idea of "union" were the most active pickets. Their commitment, again, was not to the general acceptance of the union alone. The idea of "union" meant commitment to co-workers whose opinions counted the most. It was as if the pickets were fighting more *for* someone than *against* somebody.[5]

Picket line violence, at least as compared to some events in the 1930's, has largely disappeared from the American scene. But the potential for violence is always present when an employer tries to continue production by encouraging workers to cross a picket line. An otherwise peaceful strike then may easily and quickly produce violence. The antagonism between company and union may become transformed into a personal antagonism between individuals and groups in face-to-face contact. Up to this point, the union as well as the company may be only relative abstractions to the worker. But with the appearance of workers who seek to cross a picket line, the conflict between abstractions is reduced to a personal struggle between individuals acting to defend the integrity of their group. The intensity of feeling and the potential for open hostility is greatly increased as the union-management dispute is focused upon the behavior of specific persons. The substantive differences between the union's demands and the employer's offer as collective bargaining issues may be readily displaced. The conflict may take on a new and different dimension as the strikers are integrated into a more tightly knit group to oppose the external threat of the "scabs." The picket line may then become a symbol of the group's integrity, and its defense becomes an end in itself. The larger union-management conflict may be relegated, at least for the time being, to a subordinate role and may not be brought to the fore again until the strike is ended.

---

[5] A related finding was made by Shils and Janowitz in their study of the German Army during World War II. The authors concluded that values involved in political and social systems or ethical schemes do not have much impact on the determination of a soldier to fight to the best of his ability and to hold out as long as possible. For the ordinary German soldier, the decisive fact was that he was a member of a squad or section which maintained its structural integrity and which coincided roughly with the social unit which satisfied some of his primary needs. He was likely to go on fighting, provided he had the necessary weapons, as long as the group possessed leadership with which he could identify himself, and as long as he gave affection to and received affection from the other members of his squad or platoon. In other words, as long as he felt himself to be a member of his primary group and therefore bound by the expectations and demands of its members, his soldierly achievement was likely to be good. The desire to avoid "letting the other fellow down" was one of the most important of all factors in maintaining the combat effectiveness of the soldier. Shils and Janowitz, pp. 280-315.

8

New Relationships

It has long been a basic sociological postulate that conflict is one of the substances out of which society is built.[1] It is a basic type of social interaction which produces or modifies communities of interest, unifications of individuals and groups, and organizations. Among other functions, conflict establishes the identity of groups within a social system by strengthening group consciousness, thereby contributing to the maintenance of the total social system through the creation of a balance between its various divergent interest groups. When an existing social structure is considered by its members as no longer able to provide for their needs, individuals with similar perceptions and objective positions constitute themselves into self-conscious interest groups and, through conflict, either covert or overt, seek to modify the structure. New relationships are produced; new norms and identifications are yielded; new or modified goals, values, and interests are established; and new power relationships are formed within and between groups.

Not all types of conflict are beneficial to the structure of the group or to the larger society of which the group is a part. If the contending parties no longer share the basic values upon which the legitimacy of the system itself rests, manifest conflict may disrupt the system to the point where it is actually destroyed. "Whether internal conflict prom-

---

[1] See Simmel, *passim*.

ises to be a means of equilibration of social relations or readjustment of rival claims, or whether it threatens to 'tear apart,' depends to a large extent on the social structure within which it occurs."[2]

The factory as a social system and the ethic of private property as it has developed in the United States permit wide latitude for conflict to occur without destroying the basic mutual dependence of employee and employer. There is always the possibility that overt worker-employer conflict, if sufficiently intense and prolonged, may be resolved by the dissolution of the common enterprise upon which both sides are, in the last analysis, dependent. This did not occur in the mill strike, although the organizers feared that it might. The perceived need by both the responsible union and company officials to continue the enterprise and the actual possibility of doing so forestalled this extreme development.

In Saylor, the mill strike may be seen to have achieved more of an integrative than a destructive function, although, in some ways, it achieved both. Neither the strikers nor the union directly challenged Tom Miller's fundamental right of ownership of the factory, or many of his basic rights to manage it. However, they did challenge his right to manage it at his sole discretion, and they challenged the system of authority upon which that right rested. As a result of the strike, both his authority and the system within which he exercised it were altered without destroying the mutual interdependence of the workers and their employer.

The strike, in one way or another, affected the whole community of Saylor. Without doubt, it had a profound impact upon the workers' relationships with each other, with their employer, with other union people in town, and, in some cases, with their own families. Interviews showed that other Saylor employers came to view Tom Miller in a new light as a result of the strike. Relationships between these employers and the unions with which they bargained were, in some cases, strained because of the events at the mill.

Before the strike, many of the workers were friends and neighbors outside as well as inside the mill. During the strike some associations which had been merely casual developed into warm, firm friendships. Other friendships were broken off with a great deal of bitterness and

---
[2] Coser, p. 152.

ill feeling on both sides. The strikers became a strongly unified group, set off by their common feelings and perceptions of the employer and the non-strikers. On the other side the non-strikers also looked to each other for support against the antagonisms of the striking workers.

After the strike ended (at the time the systematic interviewing was done), the work force was sharply divided and the atmosphere in the mill was tense. The strikers still considered the non-strikers as enemies and viewed them with suspicion. Most of them blamed the employer and those who had worked during the strike "for all our troubles." Some refused to speak to the non-strikers; others favored punitive measures, such as extremely high initiation fees if the non-strikers should decide to join the union at some future time.

One worker pointed out that the non-strikers had hurt him and that he would not forget it. Another said she wanted to "get my hands around their necks." Most of them felt that the non-strikers had betrayed them.

I have no use for them. They're no good for the working man. They are workers, but they don't stick with their own group. If they ever come into the union, they will never be good members. They probably would just snoop around and run to the boss and tell him everything.

A few of the strikers thought that the union should have insisted that the non-strikers be furloughed by the company as a condition of settling the strike.

I don't think that they should ever have been let into the mill after the strike. We took a loss for sixteen weeks, and they're still working even though they worked during all that time. They should have been laid off for some time. If they had not gone in, the strike would have ended that much sooner. They think the employer is a real friend, but they'll find out they won't get nothing.

The leaders were less inclined to cling to their resentments. They felt that the strength of their young union would, in large measure, depend upon uniting all of the workers. One leader commented:

I didn't think much of them. As a matter of fact, I hated them. I held it against them that they weren't seeing what the company was doing to them. All the humiliation they were willing to take, and they tore down the reputation of the city by not being good citizens and provoking all the trouble. But I don't have any hard feelings now. My ambition is to get them in the union. I always felt that they were misinformed, and it takes a long time for them to catch on.

The fence-sitters, more than the leaders or rank-and-file strikers, were ambivalent toward the non-strikers. They were apt to justify the non-strikers' attempts to work, while at the same time they tended to hold them responsible for the length of the strike. This seeming contradiction stemmed from their own peculiar positions; they were most like the non-strikers in their attitudes toward Tom Miller and their dependence upon their jobs, but, unlike the non-strikers, they were strongly influenced by union members. Thus, they could identify, at least in part, with both groups; they sympathized with the reasons the "scabs" had for working while they resented their having done so. One fence-sitter said:

They should have stayed out. That would have made things easier for all of us. There wouldn't have been the trouble there was. The strike lasted so long because of them. But I don't bother myself about them and I don't have no grudge against them.

Other fence-sitters were more openly sympathetic.

A lot of those people felt that they just had to work. I never hold anything against them for going in, but I just couldn't figure out how they could take all the abuses and name-calling. The biggest share of them were widows and other people with families who had to work.

Because the strike turned out to be more than simply the act of quitting work, the problem of building and sustaining *esprit de corps*[3] among the strikers became important. The organizers had aroused the interest of the workers and had urged them to participate in the movement. But the feelings of intimacy and closeness, the *esprit de corps,* were generated on the picket line. The non-members who persisted in efforts to work became the "enemy" upon whom blame for the strike could be laid; they were the scapegoats for all the strikers. The informal fellowship of the picket line, the singing, dancing, costumes, joking, and "having fun" brought the strikers into a close

---

[3] This term is used here in the sense given by Herbert Blumer, "Collective Behavior," in *New Outlines of the Principles of Sociology,* pp. 205-8. *"Esprit de corps* might be thought of as the organizing of feelings on behalf of the movement. In itself it is the sense people have of belonging together and of being identified with one another in a common undertaking. Its basis is constituted by a condition of rapport."

relationship where they came to know one another as human beings instead of institutional symbols of the factory. The more formal behavior in the frequent closed meetings, mass meetings, and huge demonstrations engendered a sense of vast support for their cause. The slogans, songs, and expressive gestures aimed at the non-strikers served as symbols of their common feelings. The striking workers achieved a sense of solidarity through these "secular rituals."[4]

In general, the strikers were most impressed by the feeling of belonging they developed during the strike, contrasting it always with their former impersonal and often competitive relationships. Indeed, workers pointed out that they really did not have a union before the strike. For such workers, the meaning of "union" was synonymous with a sense of solidarity with co-workers and a new appreciation of cooperative effort. A picket said:

The strike brought all of us closer together. We got to know each other and understand about our problems in the mill now that we have a chance to know each other.

This feeling of intimacy with fellow strikers was expressed by a majority of the strikers.

Now, after the strike, everybody is so much nicer with each other. You can talk to everybody, except the scabs of course. I don't know why, but they are so much more sociable and nice and friendly. It's maybe because they now know each other. Before the strike, you never had a chance to meet even those who worked with you in the same department except only casually.

I notice a big change in the people since the strike. They are more together now, they stick together. Before that, you used to sit at the same table and you wouldn't even say "hello" to the girl next to you.

Unquestionably, such feelings emerged as a result of picket line experiences.

---

[4] Warner analyzed the development of solidarity among the striking shoe workers of Yankee City: "The solidarity was achieved through the various 'secular rituals' we have mentioned; speeches by which workers' sentiments were reiterated to them in union terms; parties, entertainments, flag waving, bands and 'can days,' all designed to produce a festive spirit of comradeship; committees, picketing and parades to make the workers feel they were doing something to accomplish their ends. By all these forms of participation, union officials influenced workers to *feel* their unity and their opposition toward all owners." Warner and Low, p. 40.

The first days of picketing activity and the efforts of the union members to prevent non-strikers from entering the plant contributed more than anything else to the emergence of strong group cohesiveness. A unifying orientation developed, and the relatively unorganized behavior of the strikers became solidified and determined. The intense interaction on the picket line involved many union members who had been hesitant and confused and drew them into the ranks of the strikers. Workers who had been regarded by their fellows as mild-mannered and even meek joined the picket line and behaved in totally unexpected ways. Many of the women exhibited great courage in their determination to protect the line.

The often spontaneous and, during the first days of the strike, crowd behavior of the striking workers had a pronounced effect upon those members who were still hesitant — who had "just gone along to see what was going on." Once they became subjectively involved, they found themselves in situations which tended to polarize their feelings rapidly. Events which contributed the most to the formation of the group and to group consciousness were experienced spontaneously in the crowds which gathered at the strike scene, the mass meetings which were held, and the incidents of violence which occurred. During the course of these activities, more and more strikers were drawn into the orbit of influence of the already determined leaders. The daily efforts to keep the non-strikers out of the mill, the noisemakers, the mirrors, smokemakers, songs, parades, and other devices stirred up feelings repeatedly and maintained intense intercommunication among the strikers. For the women especially, picket line experience was unique; it interrupted the routine of their daily lives, and they were encouraged to persist in their behavior when they found themselves the most talked about and publicized group in the community.

As the union members became more and more involved in the conflict, they developed increasingly changed views of their situation. Different explanations for behavior, new criticisms, and new justifications were supported by leadership authority and group consensus and became means by which the individual could influence others as well as himself. In this way, the idea of a strike, at first rejected by many workers and feared by most, became more acceptable.

In spite of these new influences upon the relationships between workers, conflicting reactions persisted. Fear of losing a job was an important factor which prevented a number of workers from accepting the idea of a strike. However, under the influence of the union leaders, this factor, too, received a new interpretation oriented toward strike action. Many workers came to feel that the employer now considered their joining the union as a betrayal of his trust and that only a union contract could protect them from recrimination.

Yet, for a movement to succeed in the face of adversity, it must command a more persistent and fixed loyalty. This is yielded by the development of morale, thought of as an enduring collective purpose. A prolonged strike requires a degree of unity which extends far beyond the act of quitting work. Efforts of the employer to induce defections from the ranks of the strikers, the persistence of the non-strikers, the intervention of civil authorities were severe tests for the enthusiasm initially associated with the strike. Economic deprivation, coupled with the appearance of "scabs" or strikebreakers and the tactics of an employer determined to break the strike, has caused many moves toward unionization to collapse. In the Saylor case, the non-strikers proved to be a valuable asset as well as an obstacle for the union organizers.

Morale, like unity, is aided by attack upon a group. Attack intensifies anger toward the opponent and devotion to one's own fellows. It arouses feelings of resentment and provides a reinforcement for such feelings. Phil deliberately provoked the police to achieve this purpose. Efforts by the employer, the law enforcement agencies, the court, and the non-strikers to attack the picket line transformed it into a symbol of the group itself. Over and over again, the strikers, like Tom Miller and community representatives, were most impressed by the pickets and their behavior. The bonds of solidarity were forged on the picket line. A picket captain summarized the experience:

I never thought that the girls could turn out the way they did and stick to it the way they did. I thought they would stop after a week or so, but as time went on, we got stronger and stronger. The company would do a lot of things that would make the girls that much madder until they said that they would walk all winter if they had to.

Another leader spoke in similar terms:

They were brought to court, went to jail; they were out there in bad weather and good weather. I think they got more determined and militant when they saw that the company wouldn't negotiate and when the scabs went in.

In somewhat different words, a rank-and-file striker expressed the same idea:

Meeting all the girls on the line impressed me the most. I never knew them before — not really. We were all together and jolly on the line. We would dance together, sing together, and we are friends now.

This spirit also had some impact upon those who worked in the kitchen. The fence-sitters often mentioned how much they enjoyed meeting people, playing cards, and cooking for the strikers.

Solidarity sometimes was put to a test as the conflict wore on. At first, most workers believed that the strike would be short; the organizers shared this conviction. However, when the injunction was granted and efforts to bar the non-strikers were prohibited, it became evident to all that the strike would last a good deal longer than anticipated. At times the morale of the strikers ebbed — for example, when the employer was successful in his initial efforts to import coal or when skirmishes with police resulted in temporary defeats. Incidents such as these were discouraging to the pickets. Sometimes feelings of hopelessness resulted from sheer physical exhaustion brought on by constant day and night vigilance on the picket line.

Whenever the organizers felt that morale was becoming a problem, they would call mass meetings of all strikers in the union kitchen. Phil would talk to them, offering words of encouragement.

Phil would tell us that the longer it went on, the stronger we would have to be. He told us not to let down. He would tell us that we were gaining so much, that we couldn't see it all the time but that he was in many other strikes and he could tell.

As the strike progressed, the strikers developed respect, and in some cases genuine admiration, for the organizers:

I think we felt let down sometimes just from being tired. But Phil would encourage us lots of times. He told us that he knew we would win. He told us we were doing good work. He was marvelous — so patient and a wonderful speaker, and such a personality!

The impact of the strike upon those who left their jobs to join the picket line can be summarized in the words of a striker who learned the meaning of "union" only as a result of the strike.

I really don't think we had a union, not much of it anyway, before the strike. We became one with the strike, and we got stronger throughout. I mean that the people wanted a union, but it was sort of wishy-washy. If the boss gave a speech, many would believe him. And then they turned around again and believed the union. Then during the strike they really learned what it was to stick together and what they were fighting against.

In great measure, the organizers maintained morale by broadening the conflict to include not only the mill workers but a large segment of the community as well. After the United Labor Committee and public meetings and demonstrations were organized, the strike took on something of the character of a mission whose purpose, for many people, was to alter substantially the existing power relationship in the community. The moral and physical aid which the strikers received helped convince them that their cause was "just" and "right" and provided them with a new and powerful moral sanction for their picket line behavior.

We got a lot of help, a lot of moral and actual support. That's what we really needed. They used to walk the picket line with us. I felt wonderful about that because we knew we were not fighting alone and that everybody was behind us. It made a world of difference to us.

Other strikers, especially those whose prior experience with the union movement had been meager, stressed the solidarity of workers.

The unions sure stick together, and like I said, they stuck it out for the working people. It makes you feel good to see that working people really stick together.

THE NON-STRIKERS

Detailed descriptions of experiences of the few non-strikers who were interviewed might give some clues to the immediate effects of the strike on them. The mill's only truck driver, for example, was the target of a great deal of verbal abuse during the four months of the strike. Strikers, shouting "scab," followed him whenever he left the mill in his truck. He became identified throughout the town as a nonstriker, and many of his former friends and some of his close relatives completely ostracized him during the strike and for many months thereafter.

I can't go anywhere in town any more because they all know me — all over the place. When I would make my parcel post deliveries or some pick-up in the company truck, these women in cars would follow me wherever I went and yell at me and call me names. Everybody in town knows who I am and that I worked during the strike. My relatives don't have anything to do with me now!

He resigned from his bowling and softball teams soon after the strike began.

The other guys gave me the cold shoulder. They can't even be fair in sports. What's that got to do with unionism? They don't even work in the mill. . . . A guy in the next alley who was on my [bowling] team called me a scab — yelled it out loud so everybody in the place could hear him and yelled real loud that he wouldn't bowl with no scab. Some of my friends on the team told me not to pay any attention to him. But I resigned because it was just causing the few friends I had left on the team a lot of trouble and embarrassment.

He claimed that he had more enemies than friends in town.

People I don't even know and never heard of know that I worked during the strike and look at me funny when I go someplace. I don't understand it. It used to hurt, but you just turn a deaf ear and don't pay no attention after a while. It all goes in one ear and out the other like there was nothing between your ears at all.

He lived with his wife and young child in the upstairs apartment of a house owned by his father, a union member in another factory.

My father is a union man in the glove factory, and they were throwing paint at the house and nails in the driveway. He called the president of his union and told him that there was nothing in the Constitution of the United States that said he had to know whether or not a man was a union member before he rents out a place to him in his home.

There were many times, he said, when the non-strikers talked about abandoning their opposition to the union.

Many times the people got discouraged and scared for their safety, and we would talk about it amongst ourselves that maybe the union would win and then what would be the use of going on like this when we'd only have to join the union sooner or later anyhow. But the more they called us names, the more determined we got. The more they abused us, the more we didn't want to give in to them. We talked about it amongst ourselves, and after the first couple of weeks when they started to get rough, we felt we didn't want to have nothing to do with people like that. We just got madder and madder and more determined. I wanted to swing at some of them when I was driving the truck or going to work. But what would that have gotten me? All of them would have been on me, and maybe I would have punched one of them, but they would have broken my neck. We decided amongst ourselves not to say anything to them that would get them more riled up. Just because they treated us that way, we didn't have to come down to their level and treat them the same way.

He added that he had always been treated fairly by the mill's manager and could not understand the behavior of the strikers.

Tom Miller is a nice guy. Always said "hello" to me and everyone else before the strike. He's always been fair with me. The Millers made a lot of money here in this town years ago, and some people who went on strike took it out on Tom for things that maybe happened to them twenty-five years ago. That's no way to act — things in the past are in the past and that's that. I don't care how they made their money — that's none of my business. I would have done whatever they did to make all that money if I had a chance, and wouldn't you? The people said during the strike that they were out to break the Millers in this town. It had nothing to do with a union from the way some of them talked. Phil Draper stopped me on the street one day and asked me how long I've lived here. I told him all my life, and then he said, "Aren't you tired of having the Millers run your life and this town?" I told him that I didn't know who was running the town, but if it was the Millers, I'd rather have them run it than him and his union.

Several times during the strike Phil or one of the other organizers asked him to stay away from the mill.

Phil told me that if I'd only stay home, the strike would be over in a couple of weeks, and then we could all come back to work and it would all be peace and quiet again. He told me that as long as Tom Miller knew that he had some people who were willing to work, he'd hold out. I told Phil that it was my right to work or not as I saw fit and that I didn't ask him to come up here and do anything for me. I didn't invite him here and I don't tell him how to run his strike, so why does he tell me what to do with my life and why does he try to run my job. But I don't harbor no hard feelings for the organizers; that's their job, and Phil did a bang-up job of keeping those pickets all excited and riled up. He knows every trick in the book and then some.

Another non-striker related similar experiences. His brother, a union member who lived in another city, visited him shortly after the strike began and talked to him for several hours, trying to persuade him not to work. As a result, he said, "There's bad feeling between us now." His son, a member of a different union in another local factory, refused to talk to him during the strike. A cousin, with whom he was very friendly before the strike, came to the picket line several times and marched and sang with the strikers. They had not spoken to each other since, he added. A former co-worker who became a leader of the strikers had been a very close friend for many years, but when work was resumed after the strike settlement, they spoke to each other only in the course of their work relationship.

He resented the strikers and could not understand how people who had worked for the company for so many years could turn against their employer. He described at length how the strikers had harassed him. Someone painted the letters " S C A B " in bright red across the side of his white garage. Several times his tires were punctured by nails and tacks which had been thrown in his driveway. Once, when he called the gas station where he had traded for many years and asked the attendant to send someone to fix the tire, "they told me to fix it myself because they didn't want to lose any business because of me."

During the first weeks of the strike he went to his regular barber for a haircut. It was a union shop, he noted.

There was a striker sitting in one chair and a fellow I knew for many years in the other chair. This friend of mine works in the paper mill and belongs to the union over there. Well, when the striker got up to leave, he saw me but didn't say a word. I sat down in his chair, and then when my friend who works in the paper mill was finished, he got up from his chair and came over to mine and said to me, "How does it feel to sit in the chair of a union member? Why don't you go to the scab barber and get a haircut?"

He and his wife were both harassed no matter where they went around town during the strike. They gave up the pleasure of the Friday night fish-fry in the tavern where they had always gone because they were insulted by other patrons. During one of the Friday night demonstrations staged by the United Labor Committee around the Miller Department Store, he and his wife were in the store shopping.

Some of the strikers were standing across the street, and they saw me coming out. The way they started calling us names for having shopped in the store, we didn't think we'd get away from there alive.

The noisemakers, mirrors, and smoke barrels used by the pickets were very annoying, he said.

Mr. Miller brought in a bunch of radios and we listened to those all day, and it took our minds off the strike and the noise. But we were like a big family during the strike. We would go downstairs in the mill and have coffee two or three times a day and sit around and joke about it. After a while we got used to them and it didn't bother me so much. They could call up all hours of the night and yell "Scab" into the telephone and then hang up. They threw eggs full of paint at the house and broke some windows. But Mr. Miller would hire a man to fix the windows.

The strike was caused, in his opinion, by the union's chief organizer, "That Draper, the agitator, that Communistic Bolshevik."

Other non-strikers reported that they were followed and called names, that their homes were splattered with paint, and that former friends no longer spoke to them. One non-striker was amazed at the behavior of the pickets, many of whom he had known as very quiet and unassuming individuals.

Those women acted just like a bunch of stampeding cattle. One girl who always walked around in the mill with her head down, very meek and very shy — why I never could possibly imagine that she would act the way she did on the outside there. Maybe she was saving it up for all those years. Why she acted like a wild woman, and when the strike ended, she came back in the mill and now she walks around just like she used to — with her head down and so mild and meek and shy. When you'd see one or two of them downtown alone, they wouldn't even look at you. But when six or seven of them got together, they'd do almost anything. They acted just like a bunch of animals who followed their leader — that Draper.

He, like other non-strikers, reported that the noisemakers ceased being a problem for those in the mill.

We had the machines running all the time and they made a lot of noise, and we had all those radios going and we didn't take no notice of the noise at all after a while. They would yell at us when we came to work in our cars and when we went home, but that didn't bother us after a while either. It just became so much noise. You couldn't tell what they were yelling or who they were yelling at. It was just like going to a baseball game; you hear the noise of the crowd and it's just so much noise and you don't notice it after a while.

He defended the Millers, pointing out that they were employers who did not lay off their workers during slack periods.

They were always trying to help people who lived here by giving them jobs and giving them credit in the store and selling things cheap where we could save some money.

During the strike, he said, one of the strikers told him that it was time for everybody in town to get together to

put the Millers in their place. They've been running this town too long. I told this guy that I knew they had a lot to say in town, but if it was true they ran the place, then I was satisfied because they certainly had done a good job of it and if he didn't like it, why didn't he move out of town and let those who were satisfied have it as it is.

He resented the role the Mayor played during the strike and accused him of being in sympathy with the union and the strikers.

I've known him for an awful long time, and one day I went down to his office to see him to complain about the noise they were making. I knocked on his door and he let me in. "Who do you want to see?" he asked me. I told him I wanted to see the Mayor. "Well, you're looking at him and you know it." Then I said, "Are you the Mayor? I thought Phil Draper was the Mayor now." I told him about the noise and that he wasn't doing anything about it. I asked him how much money he was getting paid by Draper to help the union. He practically threw me out of his office. We won't forget things like that when election time rolls around again.

It is interesting to note that many of the same kinds of factors which generated *esprit de corps* and morale among the strikers seemed to act upon the non-strikers in the same way. They, too, became a unified, cohesive group — "one family" — as a result of their common experiences both inside and away from the mill. The abuses which they suffered tended to arouse emotions of hatred and anger toward the strikers and righteousness and sacrifice among themselves. For them, the strikers were the out-group. Their morale was sustained by the protection given by the law enforcement agencies; the new and favored treatment by their employer and the new in-group sentiments which emerged as a result of common and intense experiences all contributed to their unity and persistence.

These experiences of a few of the non-strikers are not to be taken as typical. Nor is there reason to assume that they were atypical. At minimum, they give some indication of the immediate impact of the strike upon those people who remained outside of the ranks of the union.

OTHER EMPLOYERS

Other employers in Saylor reacted against hostilities that had been generated in the community. These other businessmen did not support the strikers or the union, but they were disturbed because the strike produced tensions in other factories, divided the community, and strained its finances.

Managers of absentee-owned plants, in particular, were critical of the Millers' attitude toward the union. One called them "feudal outcasts" and added that the mill was considered to be an enterprise ruled by a family of "feudal landlords." Another said:

Miller was opposed to the union because of nineteenth century labor policies. Money demands were not a factor. Authority was the factor. They ran the mill like paternal despots.

One personnel manager commented that workers in other plants became more conscious of their roles as union members as a result of the dramatic struggle carried on by the mill women. Grievances increased and were more difficult to settle. Tardiness and absenteeism also increased as other union members spent time on the picket line at the mill. The names of non-strikers posted on union bulletin boards in other factories kept the conflict constantly on the minds of these other union members. In many cases, the non-strikers were their close friends, neighbors, or relatives.

Other employers viewed the United Labor Committee with alarm. Many points of friction developed between unions and the absentee-owned companies with which they bargained, and otherwise "peaceful" relationships tended to become strained. These bargaining relationships had produced tangible benefits for both employees and employers and were viewed as the standard for the community. Personnel and labor relations supervisors were inclined to feel that the owners of the mill should sell the enterprise to outside interests if they could not or would not bring themselves to deal with the union.[5] A supervisor in another factory said:

The Millers don't really care about this town and the people here. They're just out for themselves. I think it would be a better town if they'd sell all their holdings and move to hell out of here. They've never done this town any good that I can see.

A leading businessman reported that the Millers successfully blocked the establishment of a new industry in Saylor shortly after World War II.

They have always been considered to be the scions of the community, but they haven't done as much for the town as they should have done. They think that they are the big shots here and we are the little fellows, and that nothing we could do or would do could affect them. If we could have gotten $25,000 together to put up a building for this company, it would have been a real boost to the community. But they just wouldn't go along — wouldn't contribute anything.

The Mayor confirmed this report.

This whole area has been a notoriously low-wage area. That was started by the lumber kings, and the Millers continued it when the timber ran out. Lots of times new industries wanted to come in here, but in order to locate here a new company has to be able to get bank credit and help from other businessmen. But when you've got members of the same family sitting on the boards of the two biggest banks in town and they don't want any competition, the first thing they do when a new industry wants to come in is to find out what wages they want to pay and try everything to keep them out. It's always been known up here that the Millers pay low wages, and they didn't have any competition at all until about a dozen years ago when Sears came in with a mail order store. They had the merchandising trade in the whole area in their hands. They give credit to all kinds of people and to the farmers around here and then get them all tied up with them so they can't buy anywhere else.

---

[5] This kind of sentiment is quite different from that reported by Warner, *op. cit.* The Yankee City strike was caused in part by the shift of the shoe plant from local to absentee ownership. In Saylor, working conditions in the absentee-owned plants were considered by a large part of the community as the standard to which the mill owners should conform, a standard which the local employer resented and rejected.

THE STRIKERS AND THEIR EMPLOYER

While relations among all those involved in the conflict began to change rapidly with the beginning of the strike, perhaps the greatest change was in the strikers' view of their employer. He had hunted and fished with many of them. Others had been guests on his boat. They had enjoyed his annual Christmas parties and had looked forward to the yearly bonuses he had distributed.

Before the union was organized in his plant, Tom Miller regarded his workers as loyal and friendly to him.

We were just one big happy family before this thing started. I called 95 per cent of the employees by their first names. They were people that I knew all my life.

The workers, in turn, generally respected and in some cases admired their employer. Most of them called him by his first name: "Tom was always a very nice guy. . . . He seemed to treat everybody nice, and he always had a friendly 'hello.'" But they joined the union, despite their admiration for him, and blamed their dissatisfactions on the floorladies and other supervisors. Thus, at first, they did not define their affiliation with the union as a step involving opposition to their employer.

But as Tom Miller countered the activities of the union and made known his opposition to it, the workers came to feel that he was putting unreasonable obstacles in their path, and they became more willing to listen to the union leaders. A member of the local negotiating committee became disillusioned with him as a result of the position he took in bargaining sessions: "I used to have a lot of respect for him. But I turned against him when I watched him during negotiations. For me, he showed his real face then." This woman was not only a member of the core group in the union but was, at the same time, a leader in her department.

She (and other leaders) kept her departmental constituents informed about the progress of negotiations and their employer's position. A rank-and-file member responded:

I never thought our big boss could be so dirty. I always liked him, thought he was a fine man. But after May told us how he acted in meetings during negotiations, I couldn't think much of him any more. All the money he gave to lawyers he could have given to the workers.

Many workers became disillusioned and disappointed when Tom Miller spoke out openly against the union:

I haven't got the respect for Mr. Miller that I used to have. He's for himself and don't care for nobody else. We seen that during the strike. Before the strike, when the union was just organizing, he would give us long speeches inside the mill, and he would say that he didn't care for himself if there was a union there or not, that it didn't make any difference to him personally, and that whatever the majority of the people wanted was all right with him, though he did say that in his opinion we would be better off without a union. We found out he wasn't looking out for what the majority of the people wanted at all. He tried everything he could to keep the union out of there.

Disappointment with Tom Miller's behavior often centered around his position as a leading member of the Catholic church. His efforts to block certification of the union involved the church when he contested the election on the ground that the leaflets quoting Bishop Haas were illegally distributed near the polling place. Many Catholic workers interpreted this move as a betrayal of his faith:

Everybody in this town always thought the name Miller was wonderful, that it meant helping people. I thought Tom was religious, but he used his own Church to fight the union. He tried to make it appear that the leaflet was illegal. They were about labor having the right to organize and quoting Bishop Haas. Miller said that was influencing people and was illegal. That was his own Church, and he tried to twist it. I don't think much of that, and I can't see bringing religion into something like this. Now I see that he isn't as religious as I thought.

Other Catholic workers said that during the strike they came to feel that their employer was less motivated by his faith than by economic self-interest:

I used to think Tom was a nice guy. But I learned during the strike that he don't believe in God. He believes in the almighty dollar. He just uses the Church as a front.

As time went on, the majority of the strikers, including the fence-sitters, became convinced that only the union could protect their jobs after the strike was over because "Tom has it in for us now." Many of them felt that although they might not be discharged immediately if the union failed, the employer would make conditions so uncomfortable that they would be forced to quit. One of the pickets said, "I don't think I'd ever go back in there without a union now. I'd get a worse deal than I got before because they've seen me on the picket line." A fence-sitter was sure she would lose her job without a union to protect it: "He would just get rid of you slowly, one by one. . . ."[6]

The consequences of conflict are not always foreseen or even desired. No matter how stable or unchanging social relations may appear, they are ongoing, and the latent possibility for rapid and possibly violent change is always present. When the expected does not happen and the unexpected does, the most stable-appearing relationship may be radically displaced. A crisis situation typically presents the unexpected, and it is in this situation that "the cake of custom" is broken.[7] The strike performed this function.

---

[6] Fear of retaliation by the employer was found to be an important reason for continuing aggressive leadership among a group of local union officers employed in a steel mill. See Joel Seidman, Jack London, and Bernard Karsh, "Leadership in a Local Union," *American Journal of Sociology*, LVI (November, 1950), 229-37.

[7] Cf. Everett C. Hughes, "Institutions," in *New Outlines of the Principles of Sociology*, pp. 236 ff.

9

Four Years Later

Social adjustment is a dynamic experience. Individuals living in groups engage in conflict and achieve accommodation. When differences develop among them, they become antagonistic, and varying degrees of conflict may result. But conflict cannot continue indefinitely. Contending individuals, or groups, sooner or later are forced to find a way to reconcile their differences and existing antagonisms may be mediated or disappear completely as a new unity of purpose and outlook develops. Social processes, however, do not follow a definite, positive sequence. Individuals and groups have the capacity for making less friendly as well as more friendly adjustments, and the adjustments may range from open warfare on the one hand to complete assimilation on the other.

It is especially to the state of compromise or agreement reached by parties in conflict that the term accommodation may be applied. Every society represents an organization of elements more or less antagonistic to each other but united for the moment, at least, by an arrangement which defines the rights and duties of the parties and the respective areas of action of each.[1] This accommodation may be relatively permanent or quite transitory. In either case, the accommodation, while it is maintained, yields for the individual or for the group

---

[1] Robert E. Park and Ernest W. Burgess, *Introduction to the Science of Sociology* (Chicago, 1937), p. 665.

a recognized status. In this sense, the term does not imply a complete dissolution of differences but rather a *modus vivendi* or an arrangement that, for the time being, makes possible cooperation between antagonistic elements and the restoration of equilibrium. In other words, the antagonism is temporarily regulated and disappears as overt action, even though it remains latent and may become active again as the situation changes. Cooperation is essential to any kind of social life. All societies and all social interaction, including that which exists within a factory, is governed by established social norms. Without cooperation, social life could hardly go on. In these terms, social organization is essentially an accommodation of differences through conflict.[2]

By the fall of 1955, four years after the Saylor Company strike ended, only remnants of a conflict heritage remained. The status of many of the contestants had changed, and a new order was fairly well established and accepted by the parties. Tom Miller suddenly and tragically died about ten months after the strike, and the Miller family brought in a new manager from a distant city. Many of the former "scabs" were now included among the most eager union members. A very militant striker had married a peace officer whom she met on the picket line. Two of the most active and aggressive local leaders quit their jobs at the mill, at least in part because they were not able to adjust to the new situation which required an end to the conflict. The union-management relationship was characterized by peace and cooperation, in sharp contrast to the violence of the strike. Indeed, Phil complained that he had to be careful to protect the company from its own generosity in negotiations. The union was a going concern which had been accepted by company officials as a necessary and integral part of the plant society.

Tom Miller's death shocked the entire community. An immediate reaction of some of his friends was to say that the union had killed him — that the desertion of his "loyal" employees to the union was more than he could take and that he literally died "of a broken heart." When an autopsy revealed that his death was caused by a congenital heart condition, previously undiagnosed, some townspeople felt that he

---

[2] Cooley, p. 4. "The unity of [society] consists not in agreement but in organization, in the fact of reciprocal influence or causation among its parts. . . ."

might have lived a good deal longer had he not become involved in the violence and turmoil of the strike. Allegations of this sort were unsupported by any medical evidence, and within a few weeks they were no longer heard around town.

The new plant manager, who had had almost fifteen years' experience dealing with unions in an allied industry, apparently had no difficulty in either understanding the union or getting along with its representatives. He felt that the situation could change only for the better. Moreover, his long experience on the management side of a collective bargaining relationship gave him a perspective which aided in the transition from conflict to accommodation in the mill. His greatest problem was to get the company back on a sound financial basis. The strike had been costly in a number of respects. Because the company had been unable to deliver orders for some four months, it lost several important accounts. The situation was further complicated by the fact that the "seller's market" for the mill's product was changing to a "buyer's market" at the same time as the union came into the plant. The mill manager said, however, that the wage increase won by the union did not put the firm at a competitive disadvantage in the industry since the higher wage level and labor costs were fairly standard. On the other hand, he pointed out that the atmosphere of hostility inside the plant between those who had worked during the strike and those who had not created an unstable situation which resulted in lower individual worker productivity. He reported that it was more than a year before productivity exceeded the level that existed before the union organization.

Another difficulty, he said, was raised by the supervisors who were, with few exceptions, unwilling or slow to accept the fact of unionization. "They needed more changing on how to live with the union than the workers did on how to live with the company. . . . And the supervisors were slower to change, too. They never had a lot of authority, but what they did have was pretty much diluted and they can't acquire it now." He added that during the four years following the strike, the supervisors achieved a measure of accommodation and "there's no evidence of the conflict left."

The shop chairlady, who is the local union's chief grievance negotiator, also noted that a substantial change had occurred in the positions of the mill supervisors: "They have little authority now and are really yes-men for the manager." She explained that the new plant manager settled all piecework rates rather than having the production supervisors continue to perform this function. She noted further that the relationship between the production workers and their line supervisor was much different than four years earlier: "I tell her off when she acts up and yells at the girls, and the girls fight back a lot more than they used to."

The president of the local commented on his new role.

The union has given me more confidence in myself — as a leader, I mean. I can tell off the boss if he jumps on me. Before the union I'd just say, "Yes, sir; yes, sir," and shut up. Now I tell them off. I'm also more active in my church and in some of the social clubs I belong to than I was before the union.

A steward said that the greatest change in the years following the strike was in the behavior of the mill's superintendent.

He went out of his way to be nice to the union officers. Twice he told some "scabs" to apologize to me when they insulted me. I was collecting dues, and these "scabs" threw their dues books at me and called me some names. I complained to him and he told them to behave decently. But that was some time ago.

The strike settlement provided for a union shop to become effective if a majority of the then 180 eligible workers in the bargaining unit so voted in a state-supervised election. In the election held three months after the strike ended, a total of 177 voters turned out at the polls, and 131 affirmed the union shop clause. Only forty-six were opposed. The result surprised the union officials since only 121 workers had received strike benefits. Apparently a number of the fence-sitters or perhaps even some of the "scabs" had voted for the union shop. As a result of the election, all new employees were required to join the union within thirty days of their initial employment, and old employees would have ten months to become members.

The local's membership set the union initiation fee at $25 for all non-strikers, and four or five of them had paid this amount within a month after the strike ended. About twenty-five were still not in the union when the ten months' deadline arrived. The turning point came with two events. First, Tom's death and the hiring of a new manager meant that any implied or promised benefits made by Tom to the "loyal" employees were not likely to be forthcoming. Secondly, the company paid the negotiated wage increase to all employees retroactive to the date of the strike settlement. These amounts ranged from $45 to $60, depending on base earnings classifications. The non-strikers, like all others, received back-pay checks and, in the words of a local union official, "felt very foolish when they got them." A week after Tom's death and a few days after the ten-month deadline passed, the union arranged a meeting for all non-members in the plant dining room. They were told that the initiation fee was to be reduced from $25 to $10 and that a one-week grace period would be permitted before the union would ask the management to enforce the union shop clause. A $15 refund was given to those who had already become union members at the higher fee. By the end of the week, all non-strikers were in the union.

Integration of the non-strikers into the union took more time. Even after four years, they tended to sit together at union meetings, and a few complained that the former strikers might go out of their way a bit more to be friendly. "A couple of them live right near here," a non-striker said, "and I wish they'd call me and offer me a ride to the union hall on meeting nights. But they generally don't unless I call them." The "scabs" now agreed that the union was a "good thing." Since the non-strikers were, on the whole, the highest seniority workers, they experienced more stable employment during the generally slack period following the strike. "I now work steady instead of some of the others who used to be favorites of the forelady," another non-striker commented. "There aren't any favorites any more, and we can complain and get things done like we couldn't before the union. The union says everyone gets treated alike and that's the way it really is." Other non-strikers affirmed the benefits the older workers received from the union:

I get more work than before because of my seniority. The union is a very good thing. The people are no longer slaves. Now we have rights and much more security. The bosses don't yell any more and there's no more favoritism. And the union showed the rich ones in this town that the ordinary working class of people are somebody, too. They have to pay attention to poor people — the union forces them to do that. . . . That makes you feel much more secure as a worker.

Because of their age and seniority, the non-strikers will be among the first to receive benefits from the retirement pension plan negotiated a year after the strike ended. They were most faithful about attending union meetings. "I go to all the meetings. How else would I know what's going on? I have to go to the meetings to find out," said a sixty-four-year-old non-striker.

Everyone agreed that the strike was fast becoming a legend in the community. "There's no conflict left on the surface. Oh, you still run into people in town who take issue with the way the pickets acted on the line, but that's few and far between." Even the United Labor Committee had gone out of business. One of its former officers explained that there "wasn't no reason for it anymore. It was strictly a defensive organization for helping the strikers. But it always can be revived if the need ever comes." The need had not again occurred up to 1955.

The strike is now just a memory in Saylor, and the memory is getting dimmer as the years pass. Some of the most militant strikers are gone because they could not fit into the new framework. They found it difficult to get along with the vast majority of strikers who wanted to forget the conflict, and they were unable to get along with the non-strikers and the supervisors within the new collective bargaining relationship. A local leader explained: "They didn't want to forget the strike and stop fighting. So they quit."

Tom Miller's premature death removed one of the primary combatants from the scene, and this event perhaps aided in the establishment of a union-management relationship which would permit the accommodation of the conflict groups. The view of a local union officer may be relevant here:

It was bad to have the two leading enemies in the position of having to get along in peacetime. After they had fought with each other like they did, how could you expect them to sit down at the bargaining table and be friends. Phil couldn't leave — there was nobody to do his work. It sure was tragic, but it turned out that Tom did.

The union at the Saylor Company is a going concern. Like so much of the rest of the American labor movement, it was born in strife and violence. Again, like so many of its counterparts in other industries, in other parts of the country, and in other historical eras, it has managed, together with the company with which it deals, to submerge its conflict heritage and provide an instrument for the development of an industrial government within the workplace. Its members, officers, and the new plant manager with which it deals are confident that all concerned achieved substantial positive benefits from the turbulent experience.

Appendix:
A Note on Method

In 1950, I had an opportunity to join Joel Seidman and Jack London in a research project at the University of Chicago Industrial Relations Center. We were interested in learning something about how local union leaders, the actives, and the rank-and-file members conceive of their union. The project, therefore, was directed toward shedding light on what unionism means to these members at the local level. Our financial support came from the Carnegie Corporation.[1]

We realized, of course, that any study of local unions and their members could include only a very tiny fraction of the wide range of situations found in the American system of trade unions. There were only three of us, we planned to work in a relatively untapped area, and our universe of concern was a union movement composed of more than 15,000,000 members organized into something like 90,000 local unions chartered by more than 200 national unions. And when we considered the vast heterogeneity of the American labor movement, we knew that whatever we discovered, whatever we found unionism to mean to local union members, could be offered only as very tentative findings.

Because of the tremendous size of our universe and our very limited resources, we decided that we would seek out types of local unions which clearly differed from each other and yet were representative of distinguishable types to be found in the mainstream of the labor movement. We judged, from our experience as both students of and activists in the

---

[1] See Joel Seidman, Jack London, Bernard Karsh, and Daisy L. Tagliacozzo, *The Worker Views His Union* (Chicago, 1958).

labor movement, that one of the types certainly should be a local of workers organized in the soft goods industries, an important segment of American enterprise and of American trade unionism.

We had already begun drawing a sample of soft goods workers in the Chicago area, when the vice-president of the international union in charge of the Midwest region told us about a strike which the international union was carrying on in a small city some distance north of Chicago. In his words, the strike was a classic instance of the kind of union-management conflict which was characteristic of the industry at an earlier time. We decided immediately that this strike presented a rare opportunity to study an important aspect of the trade union movement — overt industrial warfare as a dynamic process.

The union officer assured us that we could count on the union's cooperation if we should decide to make the study, and he put us in touch with Phil Draper, the highest union official directly involved in the strike at Saylor. But before we committed ourselves to this study and abandoned our work with the group in Chicago, we wanted to know more about the Saylor strike. We wrote some exploratory letters to Phil and talked to him by phone. On the basis of this additional information, we concluded that the events in Saylor were indeed worthy of study and that we could probably get the kind of cooperation we needed from the local union, its leaders, and members.

The strike was then in its fourth month, and negotiations were under way which led to the settlement. Before it ended, however, I was able to visit Saylor to take a first-hand look at the situation. I spent many hours with Phil listening to him describe in detail the background and present status of the strike, and he also arranged for me to meet with the local leaders. They seemed genuinely flattered that an outsider wanted to come several hundred miles to learn something about what they were doing, and they were more than happy to cooperate.

During these first conversations, I learned about the bitterness which had developed between the strikers and those who were working during the strike. This made me quite certain that it would not be easy to reach the latter group. Nor could I be sure that the employer would tell me his views and experiences. Nonetheless, my colleagues and I concluded that we would begin the study and try to establish contact with the nonstrikers and the mill management after we had arrived at the scene to do the field work.

By this time we had enough information to define a series of problem areas around which to construct a preliminary interview guide. The guide, which contained some sixty items, was tested on six rank-and-file strikers whose names were drawn randomly from the universe. After we analyzed the responses, we decided either to eliminate or combine several questions on the guide which we finally used in the study.[2] All but a few of the questions were open-ended, designed to elicit qualitative responses — the experiences which the participants had and their feelings about them.

We did not think it was necessary to interview the entire universe of participants. A carefully drawn sample of the mill workers would give us, we felt, the kind of qualitative data we were seeking. Further, our exploratory study had led us to conclude that the mill workers probably would be quite homogeneous since they had all participated intimately in a profoundly collective endeavor and had all shared the same kinds of objective experiences. However, since we wanted types or patterns of experiences in terms of quality, we were prepared to interview as long as we felt we were discovering new types.

By the time we completed the study design and made all other arrangements for our field work, the strike had been settled. Our universe of concern, at this point, was the 156 workers then on the mill payroll who had been employees when the organizing drive started. For purposes of sampling, we divided the universe into four sub-universes:

(1) The leadership group was defined as all elected local officers, including executive board members and shop stewards — thirteen individuals in all. Without exception, these respondents also had been members of either the inside organizing committee or, later, the negotiating committee. We interviewed 100 per cent of this group.

(2) The rank-and-file group was defined to include all workers, excluding leaders, who had joined the union prior to the strike and had remained members in good standing. Eighty-two persons were in this group. Their names were arranged alphabetically by last name, and every other name was selected. Thus, forty-one rank-and-file members were drawn for the sample. We systematically interviewed the first sixteen persons on this list. However, interviewing was halted when it appeared that this sub-universe was extremely homogeneous in responses to the interview questions, and a sub-sample of the remaining twenty-five was drawn by again arranging the last names alphabetically and choosing every fourth name. Thus, we selected seven additional persons and interviewed each of them. No new patterns of response were discovered from among the sub-sample interviews.

(3) A sub-universe called "fence-sitters" was defined as (a) those who

---

[2] See Interview Guide, Appendix 2.

joined the union prior to the strike but subsequently withdrew only to rejoin later, and (b) those who joined the union for the first time during the strike. Union records showed that thirty-two workers fell into this category. A 50 per cent sample of this population was selected by arranging last names alphabetically and drawing every other name. We interviewed eleven of the fence-sitters, but responses began to repeat after the first six interviews. Because we were confident that the total of eleven exhausted all patterns of response, we decided not to draw a sub-sample of the remainder of the group. We contacted the remaining five in the original sample, but we did not interview them.

(4) The remaining sub-universe was made up of twenty-nine workers who did not join the union and did not respect the picket line set up by the strikers. We hoped to be able to interview the non-strikers systematically. However, it soon became apparent in the course of our field work that the violence of the strike and the bitterness between former friends and associates was such that systematic interviewing would be impossible. We were able to contact several of the non-strikers, but only five of them agreed to be interviewed. In an effort to reach more of this group, I called one of their leaders by telephone, hoping that if she would agree to an interview, the other non-strikers might follow her lead. Her first reaction to my request was somewhat hostile, but after I discussed and explained the study in some detail, she agreed to "talk to the girls and Mr. Miller and see how they feel." A few days later I spoke to her again by phone, and she answered that the non-strikers were unwilling to be interviewed even though their employer had encouraged them to cooperate. "The girls feel that things are bad enough now without stirring up anything more, and we want to let bygones be bygones," she explained. Thus, we decided that it would be best not to pursue further interviews from among this group — at least not at this time.

Other factors contributed to our decision not to press for interviews among the non-strikers. A state-supervised election for affirmation of a union shop clause negotiated in the strike settlement was scheduled, and we did not want to intercede further in an already confused and extremely tense situation fraught with conflict and suspicion between non-strikers and union members. We had been told repeatedly that the deep breach which separated the two groups of workers was just beginning to show some signs of healing, that at least some of the workers were beginning to speak to members of the other group. Our experience with depth interviewing had shown us that in the course of such an interview, while the respondent was recalling experiences she had had, her imagery of events in the recent past was again brought sharply into focus, often re-creating for her an earlier and beginning-to-be-forgotten antagonism. This had happened already in interviews with three of the non-strikers. An interview would begin with the respondent expressing few signs of emotion regarding the strikers. But by the end of the interview, she tended to describe her experiences during the strike with much more feeling and to express lasting and seemingly permanent hatred for those whom she held responsible for the events in which she was caught up.

Because of this interview effect, the coming union security election for which the union was marshalling all its forces, and the faint indications that the split between the strikers and non-strikers was beginning to heal, we felt that we did not want to be responsible for or contribute to any further antagonisms. Thus, after we had interviewed five members of the non-striker group and the spokesman for a number of others stated that her associates wanted to "let bygones be bygones," we made no further attempts to contact non-strikers at this time.

We spent many hours, over a period of six months, discussing the strike and the union organization with the organizers, Phil Draper in particular. We wire-recorded two such discussions, each of which lasted more than three hours. We did not use a set of pre-structured questions in talking to the organizers. Rather our probings took the form of general discussions on organizing strategy and the specific tactics used in Saylor.[3] By this time we had become immersed in our subject matter and could construct meaningful questions on the spot. Our aim in these discussions was to get from the responsible union officials as complete a picture as we could of the "why" and the "how" of their activities in Saylor. We were fortunate on this score for at least a couple of reasons. First, we had the complete confidence of Phil and his staff. Much earlier we learned that we had many mutual friends in the Chicago area and this fact became important in establishing the kind of rapport which we needed to understand the organizers' activities. And no less important was Phil's earlier training as an attorney. He completely understood our purposes as university-based researchers and he thoroughly appreciated the value which we saw in studying the strike as a process and making public the results of our study. In addition to being a very capable union organizer and administrator, Phil is a highly articulate person with a trained capacity to see the significance, for his purposes, of details and to talk about them lucidly and in the light of some larger purpose that he might have.

---

[3] See Robert K. Merton and Patricia L. Kendall, "The Focused Interview," *American Journal of Sociology*, LI (May, 1946), 541-57.

In addition to the union people involved, we interviewed community leaders — the Mayor, businessmen, educators, and leaders of the local trade union movement — and we picked up much additional information and expressions of viewpoint from casual conversations with a number of shopkeepers, cab drivers, barbers, and others. Of course, the mill manager also was interviewed.

Interviews with the strikers and fence-sitters lasted two hours, on the average, and were carefully recorded verbatim. Since the questions asked all related to the respondent's total experience with respect to his or her new status as a union member, we analyzed the entire interview, as an integrated whole, for content, and the categories of responses were derived empirically from the interview data. We subjected our data to quantitative measures in order to establish dominant or modal distributions with respect to such things as percentages of union members dissatisfied with issues, percentages of members who joined the union with prior union conviction or experience, percentage of members who joined essentially because of a need or desire to conform, the distribution of primary and secondary wage-earners at the time of joining, and the mean age and length of employment of the different classes of mill workers.

The results of these quantitative measures are for the most part presented in modal terms rather than as precise statistical results. This was done because, first of all, we were interested in the quality of the behavior and secondly because our total universe and the sub-samples within it were of such relatively small size as to lead us to conclude that what we could not describe and defend in qualitative terms would be no better described nor defended when presented as measures of statistical significance between variables. The quantitative manipulations we made were intended to give us clues to understanding behavior and relationships rather than as statistical proof of our findings.

Most of the respondents, with the exception of the non-strikers and some businessmen, were most willing to be interviewed. They seemed to be pleased because a professor from a famous and distant university had come a long way to seek them out and talk to them as individuals. Indeed, they were genuinely eager to tell an outsider about their experiences, particularly after they understood that the study would be published and the "outside world" would learn of their activities. The strikers had won a bitter strike during which some of them had been arrested. They had participated in violence and had developed rather heroic self-conceptions. They were proud of what they had done.

In almost all cases, we made appointments for interviews by telephone.

Those who had no phones were contacted through mill co-workers who had already been interviewed. Often, when we phoned a worker to arrange for an interview, she would respond, "Oh, yes. I know all about you, and I was wondering when you'd get around to me."

Our activities as researchers and interviewers became a topic of conversation among the union members, and we learned from time to time of workers who felt cheated because they had not been interviewed. Sometimes, at social affairs which the union sponsored during the period of our field work, members would seek us out to ask why we had not called them. If their names were on our list, we could reply that they could expect a call shortly. But if their names were not in our sample, we had to explain enough about sampling methods so that they understood they were not the objects of arbitrary discrimination. In spite of our explanations, some of them insisted on being interviewed, and we included their responses in the sample for analysis.

Interview data alone could not give us the total picture we were seeking. A great deal of information came from Phil Draper's complete union file of all matters relating to events in Saylor. This file, which he made available to me, contained more than 500 documents of various kinds: personal and official correspondence between the organizers and their union superiors; daily and weekly field reports from the organizers to the regional headquarters of the union; a complete file of correspondence between the union officers and the employer; a complete file of all letters sent by the company to the employees as well as the union's letters and leaflets distributed to the workers; correspondence between union officers and other unions in Saylor; more than 300 photographs of strikers taken at various times during the strike; a file of songs which the strikers sang on the picket line; transcripts of all court and National Labor Relations Board proceedings.

In addition, Phil gave me access to his personal file which contained outlines of his speeches, agenda and personal memoranda for bargaining sessions, notes taken on the spot during union meetings, demonstrations, mass meetings, and negotiations, personal and telephone conversations. Phil was an inveterate note-taker (stemming at least in part from his legal training), a personal characteristic of great value to a researcher who is interested in studying the process in which such a person is involved. We also obtained and analyzed a complete file of the local daily newspaper for references to the mill strike. Further, several of the strikers had kept elaborate scrapbooks which contained photographs, leaflets, news clippings, and personal mementos of their struggle. Two of these collections were given to me.

After we had completed our extended field work, I made several return trips to Saylor to check on data and to secure additional information to clarify confused or obscure points. I made my final visit about four years after the strike ended — this time to find what I could of the legacy or heritage of the conflict.

My interviewing for this purpose was in no way systematic. I visited with most of the people who had been leaders in the strike and with about a dozen rank-and-file members whom we had interviewed earlier. In addition, I called on a half dozen former fence-sitters and all of the nonstrikers previously interviewed. During this trip, I was able to talk to four more non-strikers in their homes — people whom we had not been able to interview earlier. My discussions with them turned on their present relations with their co-workers and their employer. I was also interested, of course, in learning something about their views of their union now that it was a going concern. My purpose was to get impressions which would portray accurately the transition from conflict to accommodation or cooperation.

The manuscript went through four complete drafts before its final form was fixed. A problem which continually bothered me was the need to find uncomplicated language which would be meaningful to the non-sociologist and yet explain complex concepts without doing violence to them. Also, there are many points in the story which were either unclear to me or about which I had made factual errors. Successive drafts were read by Phil for factual accuracy. The interpretations, however, are my own and though I had advice at many points, the final choice was always mine.

Bibliography

Bernard, L. L. "Crowd," *Encyclopedia of Social Sciences,* IV, pp. 612-13.

Blumer, Herbert. "Collective Behavior," *New Outlines of the Principles of Sociology.* Ed. Alfred McClung Lee. New York: Barnes and Noble, 1946.

———. "Group Tension and Interest Organizations," Industrial Relations Research Association, *Proceedings of the Second Annual Meeting.* Champaign, Ill.: The Association, 1949, pp. 150-64.

———. "Sociological Theory in Industrial Relations," *American Sociological Review,* XII (June, 1947), 271-78.

Chamberlain, Neil. *The Union Challenge to Management Control.* New York: Harper, 1948.

Commons, John R. *The Legal Foundations of Capitalism.* New York: Macmillan, 1924.

Cooley, Charles H. *Social Organization.* Glencoe, Ill.: Free Press, 1956.

Coser, Lewis A. *The Functions of Social Conflict.* Glencoe, Ill.: Free Press, 1956.

Drucker, Peter F. *The New Society.* New York: Harper, 1950.

Festinger, Leon. "The Role of Group Belongingness in a Voting Situation," *Human Relations,* II (1947), 154-80.

Gardner, Burleigh. *Human Relations in Industry.* Chicago: Richard D. Irwin, Inc., 1947.

Gouldner, Alvin W. *Wildcat Strike.* Yellow Springs, Ohio: The Antioch Press, 1954.

Hiller, Ernest T. *The Strike: A Study in Collective Action.* Chicago: University of Chicago Press, 1928.

Hoxie, Robert Franklin. *Trade Unionism in the United States.* New York: D. Appleton, 1917.

Hughes, Everett C. "Institutions," *New Outlines of the Principles of Sociology.* Ed. Alfred McClung Lee. New York: Barnes and Noble, 1946.

Hyman, Herbert H. "The Relation of the Reference Group to the Judgment of Status," *The Psychology of Status,* Archives of Psychology, No. 269, 1942.

Klineberg, Otto. *Social Psychology.* New York: Henry Holt, 1954.

LeBon, Gustave. *The Crowd: A Study of the Popular Mind.* London: T. F. Unwin, 1897.

Mayo, Elton. *Human Problems of an Industrial Civilization.* New York: Macmillan, 1933.

———, and George F. Lombard. *Teamwork and Labor Turnover in the Aircraft Industry of Southern California.* Cambridge: Harvard University Press, 1944.

Mead, George Herbert. *Mind, Self and Society.* Chicago: University of Chicago Press, 1934.

Merton, Robert K., and Patricia L. Kendall. "The Focused Interview," *American Journal of Sociology,* LI (May, 1946), 541-57.

Merton, Robert K., and Alice S. Kitt. "Contributions to the Theory of Reference Group Behavior," *Continuities in Social Research.* Eds. Robert K. Merton and Paul E. Lazarsfeld. Glencoe, Ill.: Free Press, 1950.

Millis, Harry A., and Emily Clark Brown. *From the Wagner Act to Taft-Hartley.* Chicago: University of Chicago Press, 1950.

Mills, C. Wright. *The New Men of Power.* New York: Harcourt, Brace, 1948.

Newcombe, Theodore. *Social Psychology.* New York: Dryden Press, 1950.

Park, Robert E. *Society.* Glencoe, Ill.: Free Press, 1955.

———, and E. W. Burgess. *Introduction to the Science of Sociology.* Chicago: University of Chicago Press, 1942.

Seidman, Joel, Jack London, and Bernard Karsh. "Leadership in a Local

Union," *American Journal of Sociology*, LVI (November, 1950), 229-37.

Seidman, Joel, Jack London, and Bernard Karsh. "Why Workers Join Unions," *Annals of the American Academy of Political and Social Science*, CCLXXIV (March, 1950), 75-85.

——— and Daisy Tagliacozzo. *The Worker Views His Union*. Chicago: University of Chicago Press, 1958.

Sherif, Muzafer. *Group Relations at the Crossroads*. New York: Harper, 1953.

Shils, Edward A. "Primary Groups in the American Army," *Continuities in Social Research*. Eds. Robert K. Merton and Paul E. Lazarsfeld. Glencoe, Ill.: Free Press, 1950.

———, and Morris Janowitz. "Cohesion and Disintegration in the Wehrmacht in World War II," *Public Opinion Quarterly*, XII, No. 2 (1948), 280-315.

Simmel, Georg. *Conflict*. Glencoe, Ill.: Free Press, 1955.

Stouffer, Samuel A., et al. *The American Soldier*. Princeton: Princeton University Press, 1949.

Taylor, George W. *Government Regulation of Industrial Relations*. New York: Prentice-Hall, 1948.

———. "The Strike as a Socio-Economic Institution," Industrial Relations Research Association, *Proceedings of the Third Annual Meeting*. Madison, Wis.: The Association, 1950, p. 305.

U. S. Bureau of Labor Statistics. *Analysis of Work Stoppages*, 1955, Bulletin No. 1196. Washington: Government Printing Office, 1956, p. 1.

———. *Monthly Labor Review*, LXXVII, May, 1954.

———. *Monthly Labor Review*, LXXIX, July, 1956, p. 805.

U. S. Congress. *Labor-Management Relations Act, 1947*. Public Law 101, 80th Cong., 1st Sess., 1947, Sec. 101, sub-sec. 1.

Warner, W. Lloyd, and J. O. Low. *The Social System of the Modern Factory, The Strike: A Social Analysis*. New Haven: Yale University Press, 1947.

Index

Across-the-board wage increase. *See* Wage increase
Age: reason for not joining the union, vi, 40-41, 43
American Federation of Labor: 1947 organizing drive, 18-21; 1950 preliminary survey, 21-22; 1950 organizing drive, 22-28. *See also* Retail Clerks Union; Trades and Labor Council
Arbitration: union offer to accept, 77, 78; inclusion as step in grievance procedure, 98

Back door agreements, 99-100
Bail bond provisions for strikers, 72
Behavior of individuals: influences on, 5, 35-36, 36-37, 40, 45, 107-8, 120-21
Bonus prices. *See* Piecework prices

Call-in pay, 98
"Captive audience" meetings, 50, 55, 61, 114
Catholic church: Bishop Francis J. Haas, 56; as influence on workers, 112; employer as member of, 18, 152

Catholic workers: change in attitude toward employer, 152
Causes of strikes, 2
Chamber of Commerce, 95-96
Citizens Committee, 95-96
Coal shipments: efforts to block, 90-92
Collective bargaining: control of conflict, 10, 12
Collective bargaining agreements: in effect in 1955, 1n
Community support: efforts of organizer to gain, 76, 87
Conflict: unions and management as interest groups, 11; as means of balance, 13n-14n; as social interaction, 135
Conformity: influence on individual behavior, 35-36; influence on fence-sitters, 36-37, 40, 108n
Congress of Industrial Organizations: failure of "Operation Dixie," 100; mentioned, 87
Contract negotiation meetings, 64
Craftsmen: recruiting by union organizers, 24

INDEX   173

"Crowne, Helen." *See* Union Organizers

Death benefits, 88
Department store: indirect boycott of, 88; picketing by Retail Clerks Union, 88-89
Destruction of mill property, 86
Destruction of non-striker property, 84
"Draper, Phil." *See* Union Organizers

Employee-employer relationship: expression of conflict in, 8; causes of dissatisfaction, 9-10
Employer: fear of as cause of failure of 1947 organizing drive, 21; attitude of fence-sitters toward, 38-39, 152-53; hints of reprisal, 114-15; attitude of non-strikers toward, 148; attitude of other employers toward, 149-50; attitude of strikers toward, 151-53; effect of strike on business of, 156
Employer efforts to combat unionism: withdrawal movement, 39, 52, 115; letters to employees, 46-48; "captive audience" meetings, 50, 55; unilateral wage increase, 50; objection to certification of union, 56-57
Esprit de corps: defined, 138n; growth on picket line, 138-39; among non-strikers, 148-49

Favoritism of supervisors, 22, 29, 31, 36, 55
Federal Mediation and Conciliation Service, 65, 75, 93
Fence-sitters: defined, 36-40; attitude toward employer, 37-38, 152-53; withdrawal from union membership, 39-40; tactics of organizers in dealing with, 61-62; duties during strike, 72; influences on, 106-8, 120-21; attitude toward picket line, 126-27; attitude toward non-strikers, 128, 138; attitude toward strike, 133
"Free speech" provision: use by employer under Taft-Hartley Act, 114

"Gentlemen's agreement" to prevent strike violence, 74-75
Grievance procedure, 64, 65
Group pressure: reason for joining union, 35-36; influence on fence-sitters, 36-37, 40, 107-8, 120-21; influence on non-joiners, 45; influence on decision to strike, 132-33
Guaranteed minimum wages: effect of increase on incentives, 59

Haas, Bishop Francis J., 56, 152
Health and retirement plans, 55
House calls: use by union organizers, 20, 22-23, 24, 25, 65, 106

Incentives: reduction in caused by increase in guaranteed minimum, 59
In-groups and out-groups, 109n, 112
Initiation fees, 157-58
Injunction to prevent picket line violence, 75-76, 79
"Inside" organizing committees: formation of, 26; use of meetings to maintain morale, 57; transformation into strike committee, 72; importance of, 110-11
Institutions: union organization as formation of, 6; defined, 10n
Interference with home life: cause of worker dissatisfaction, 32
International union: death benefits, 28; strike recommendation policy, 62; strike benefit policy, 67

Job classification system, 64

Layoffs, 23, 29
Leaflets: use by union organizers, 27, 55, 56-57; by Bishop Francis J. Haas, 56-57
Letters to employees: use by employer, 46-48, 53; use by union organizers, 49-50, 51, 52-53, 57
Lockouts: mechanism to force agreement, 13

Loyalty to employer: influence on fence-sitters, 37-38

Management authority: union penetration of, 10, 11, 113, 136

Mass meetings: means of maintaining morale, 142

Mass picketing, 76

Mayor: activities during strike, 70-72, 122-23; attitude of non-strikers toward, 148; attitude toward employer, 150

Membership meetings, 27, 58

Membership-withdrawal petitions, 52, 115

Methodist church: pastor as chairman of Citizens Committee, 96

Miller Brothers Department Store. See Department store

"Miller, Tom." See Employer

Mirrors: use of to harass non-strikers, 81, 147

Morale: use of meetings to maintain, 57, 142; use of rumors, 64; blocking of coal shipments as means of maintaining, 92; picket songs, 82-84; attack as instrument in developing, 141; union organizer's role in maintaining, 142-43: non-strikers, 148-49

National Labor Relations Board: petition for election, 48; date of representation election, 53; delay in certification of representation election, 56-57; denial of company objections to certification of union, 57-58; certification of union confirmed, 60-61; denial of company motion for reconsideration of decision, 64; use of machinery by employer, 113; ruling on "captive audience" meetings, 114; mentioned, 28

New Deal: mentioned, 100

Noisemakers: use of to harass non-strikers, 80-85, 147-48

Non-joiners: described, 40-41, 108; difficulty in obtaining interviews, 40; physical handicap as influence on, 41; influence of seasonal nature of industry, 42; attitude toward union organizers, 43; influence of age, 43; power of group pressure on, 45. See also Non-strikers

Non-strikers: attempts to enter mill during strike, 70-71, 72-74, 75; devices used to harass, 80-85, 125, 147-48; attitude of fence-sitters toward, 128, 138; effect on pickets, 128-29, 134; attitude of strikers toward, 137-38; as asset to union organizers, 140; effect of strike upon, 143-49; attitude toward employer, 145, 148; attitude toward union organizers, 145, 147; attitude toward picket line, 147; attitude toward Mayor, 148; esprit de corps of, 148-49; posting of names of, 149; initiation fees, 157-58; slow integration of, 158

"Operation Dixie," 100

Organizers. See Union organizers

Organizing drives: failure of 1947 drive, 18-21; 1950 preliminary survey, 21-22; secrecy in 1950 campaign, 23-24; during the thirties, 100; failure of "Operation Dixie," 100; differences between 1947 and 1950, 105; development of group feeling, 130

Organizing tactics: house calls, 20, 22-23, 24, 25, 65, 106; preservation of secrecy, 23-24; recruitment of craftsmen, 24; formation of "inside" organizing committee, 26, 110-11; distribution of leaflets, 27, 55, 56; use of income tax returns, 19-20, 27; speeches to employees, 27-28, 54-55; letters to employees, 49-50, 51, 52-53, 57; pre-election rally, 54-55; meetings of employees, 54-55; use of rumors, 64; changes in methods and techniques, 100, 117

Paid holidays, 65

Petitions to withdraw union membership, 52

Physical handicap: reason for not joining union, vi, 41, 108

Picketing: cooperation of members of other unions, 74; Retail Clerks Union, 88-89; company sales offices, 94; discussed, 121-34; attitude of fence-sitters toward, 133; effect on relationships between workers, 138-39; factor in development of group feeling, 138-39. *See also* Picket line; Picket line violence

Picket line: attempts to cross, 70-71; activities of union organizers on, 73; picket songs, 82-84; refusal of Teamsters Union to cross, 82n, 88; cooperation of other union members, 112; as factor in creating group feeling, 125-26; attitude of fence-sitters toward, 126-27; effect of non-strikers on, 128-29, 134; growth of *esprit de corps,* 138-39; attitude of strikers toward, 142; attitude of non-strikers toward, 147

Picket line violence: attempts to cross picket line, 70-71; arrest of pickets, 72-73, 74, 84-85, 86-87; memorandum of agreement to prevent, 74-75; injunction to prevent, 75-76, 79; as reduction of conflict to personal struggle, 134

Piecework prices: dissatisfaction of workers with, 22, 29-30; below level in union shops, 54; union demands for improvements in, 55; inequities in company system, 58-59; changes in system, 98, 157

Police: attempts to help non-strikers enter plant, 70, 122-23; activities during strike, 72-73, 75; jurisdictional dispute, 79-80; arrests of union members, 85-86

Post Office: coal shipments, 91

Primary groups: importance of, vii; motivation of group members, 5; defined, 5n

Primary wage-earners: fence-sitters, 36; non-joiners, 41, 107, 108

Railway Clerks Union, 91

Railway Express Company, 85, 88

Reasons for joining union: family encouragement, 34-35; previous union membership, 35; group pressure, 35-36; disorganized work assignments, 36; favoritism of supervisors, 36; insecurity of job tenure, 36; wage rates, 36

Reasons for not joining union: physical handicap, 41, 108; age, 43; previous union experience, 43-44

Representation election: petition for, 48; date set, 53; delay in certification caused by leaflet, 56-57; denial of company objections, 57-58; certification of results confirmed, 60-61; denial of company motion for reconsideration, 64

Reprisals: fear of, 23, 141, 152-53; hints of in employer statements, 114-15

Retail Clerks Union: picketing of department store, 88-89

Retirement pension plan, 159

Rumors: use in maintaining morale, 64

Saylor: history of town, 16; unionism prior to strike, 17; effect of strike on, 136-37

Saylor Company: history of firm, 17; labor force, 18; failure of 1947 organizing drive, 18-21; causes of worker dissatisfaction, 22

Scabs. *See* Non-strikers

Seasonal nature of industry: influence on non-joiners, 42

Secondary boycott ban, 88

Secondary wage-earners, vi

Seniority system, 29, 98

Seventh-Day Adventist church, 128

Sit-down strikes, 1

Slowdowns, 1

Smokemakers, 81-82, 147

Songs: device to maintain picket morale, 82-84

Strike action: response of workers to, 5-6
Strike benefits: international union policy, 67; amounts of, 72
Strike recommendation: international union policy, 62
Strikers: bail bond, 72; attitude toward strike, 118-21; attitude toward picket line, 125-26, 142; attitude toward non-strikers, 137-38; meaning of "union" to, 139; attitude toward employer, 151-53
Strikes: mechanism to force agreement, vi, 13; effects on community, x, 136-37; defined, 1, 2; frequency of, 1; general, 1; "quickie," 1; sitdown, 1; slowdowns, 1; causes of, 2; as social conflict, 3, 4, 12; alternatives to, 13; World War II, 13n; attitude of strikers toward, 118-21; as group activity, 129-30; attitude of fence-sitters toward, 133; effect on relationships between workers, 136-38, 139; effect on non-strikers, 143-49; effect on other plants, 149; changes after end of, 155-57; effect on company's business, 156
Strike settlement, 157
Strike study: methods of study, xi-xii, 4, 161-68
Strike tactics: offer to accept arbitration, 77, 78; devices to harass non-strikers, 80-85, 146; mass meetings, 87-88; blocking of coal shipments, 90-92; picketing of sales offices, 94
Strike violence. See Picket line violence
Strike vote, 67, 132-33

Taft-Hartley Act: passage, 21; cause of failure of 1947 organizing drive, 21; unilateral wage increase as unfair labor practice, 58; secondary boycott ban, 88; effect on organizing drives, 100-101, 105; machinery of National Labor Relations Board, 113; use by employer of "free speech" provision, 114

Tax returns: use by union organizer, 19-20, 27
Teamsters Union: cooperation with pickets, 82n; refusal to cross picket line, 88, 89; refusal to deliver coal to department store, 90
Trades and Labor Council: encouragement of organization at Saylor Company prior to 1947, 18; request for organizer in 1947, 18; cooperation with strikers, 74

UAW-CIO: mentioned, 24
Unfair labor practices, 58, 115
Unilateral wage increase, 58, 115
Union: meaning of to workers, 133-34, 139, 142-43
Union demands, 54, 55
Union-management relationships: conflict in, 4
Union organizers: tactics, 4-5, 7, 22-28; use of tax returns, 19-20, 27; importance of tactics and personality, 26, 104-5, 106; speeches to employees, 27-28, 54-55; attitude of non-joiners toward, 43, 145, 147; use of letters to employees, 57, 116; activities on picket line, 73; arrested, 84, 85; efforts to gain community support, 87; efforts to block coal shipments, 90-92; role in developing union sentiment, 103-4; need for imagination and flexibility, 106; creation of "enemy" symbol, 109, 110; formation of "inside" organizing committees, 110-11; membership meetings, 116; as a collective representation, 116-17; non-strikers as asset to, 140; role in maintaining morale, 142-43
Union organizing: success dependent on worker dissatisfaction, 4-5; response of workers to, 5-6; as formation of new social institution, 6; reasons why workers organize, 10; failure of 1947 drive, 18-21; 1950 preliminary survey, 21-22; secrecy in 1950 campaign, 23-24; during the

INDEX   177

thirties, 100; failure of "Operation Dixie," 100; process of, 102n; differences between 1947 and 1950, 105; development of group feeling, 130

Union security, 64, 65, 97, 157

United Labor Committee: formation of, 87; demonstrations in support of Retail Clerks Union, 89; devices to enlist aid of other union members, 112; effect on nature of strike, 143; attitude of other employers toward, 149-50; discontinuance, 159

Vacations: union demand for, 55

Violence. *See* Picket line violence

Wage increase: employer's efforts to combat unionism, 50; demanded by union, 55; granted by company after election, 58; granted by company after strike, 98. *See also* Unilateral wage increase

Wage levels: Saylor Company, 18

Wage rates: worker dissatisfaction with, 22; reasons for joining union, 29, 35, 36; below levels in union shops, 54

Wagner Act: mentioned, 100

War Labor Board: settlement of differences without strike power, 13n

Withdrawal of membership petitions, 52, 61

Work assignments: dissatisfaction with as cause for joining union, 31, 36

Worker dissatisfaction: needed for successful union organization, 4-5, 6; role of union organizer in crystallizing, 7, 103-4; causes of, 7, 9-10, 36, 102-3; favoritism of supervisors, 22, 31, 32; piecework prices, 29-30, 54-55; wage rates, 22, 29, 35, 54; lack of seniority provisions, 29; disorganized work assignments, 31; interference with home life, 32; union as unifying symbol, 129-30, 131-32